Praise for Barbara Sinor's
Tales of Addiction and Inspiration for Recovery

"*Tales of Addiction* is at once heart-wrenching and heart-warming. Filled with stories of heroic struggle, victory, and defeat, it is both illuminating and inspiring. The book is intensely personal, yet sadly universal; the stories recounted are for anyone touched by the trials of addiction."

—Rev. Steve Doolittle, Astara, Author
From the Heart: Five Minute Inspirations

"*Tales of Addiction* is about courage—the true meaning of which is essential for our world to rediscover. And nowhere is courage more necessary than facing the demons of addiction. This inspiring and penetrating new book by Dr. Barbara Sinor shows us how we gather the courage and the force of will to make a transformational change. The key is listening to (or reading) each other's stories, simply because narrative builds community, and community can be the supportive container that allows us to free ourselves from self-destructive patterns. Just from reading the stories that Dr. Sinor has collected, I can feel myself to be part of a healing community. These deeply honest and authentic personal accounts take me into my heart, reminding me how to understand and be compassionate towards addictions—not just those I encounter in others, but especially my own."

—Mark Thurston, PhD,
co-founder, Personal Transformation and Courage Institute,
author *Willing to Change: The Journey of Personal Transformation*

"Tales of Addiction is a collection of real life stories that chronicle not only the pain of addiction but also show the healing power of recovery. These heart-wrenching and ultimately heartwarming stories, provide the inspiration for each one of us to know that recovery works."

—Ken Seeley, Ph.D., *Intervention 911* Television Program,
Author, *Face It and Fix It*

"Addiction is a disease that often doesn't present itself in a form that onlookers notice; it's often hidden by the addict or his family, to a point even the closest friends and family don't know about it or even realize there is a problem. As I read each story in *Tales of Addiction* by Dr. Barbara Sinor, I felt the pain, dismay, denial, and hopelessness of each writer. Some stories are just down-right difficult to read and offered much contemplation as I reflected back on my own life and experiences. Yet, every one of the stories offers hope. The reader gets the distinct guidance that a shift happens and the addiction becomes real and many times recovery ensues. This goes for both the addict and the family member. Just because we don't have a substance addiction, it doesn't mean we aren't susceptible to enabling, which ends up being an addiction in itself. Poignant, reflective, and offering the knowledge there is hope and recovery, *Tales of Addiction* gives the reader the sense they are not alone. But most of all, the stories reflect compassion and in the end, the true identity of each person."

—Irene Watson, MA, author,
The Sitting Swing: Wisdom to Know the Difference and
Rewriting Life Scripts: Transformational Recovery for Families

"Tales of Addiction contains stories of the heart. Many people suffer from problems with drugs but they do not start out that way. In that respect, anyone is a candidate for a drug problem, however, some are able to see danger while others do not until they are in so deep that they cannot get out. The public needs to understand that we must stop blaming addicts for their addiction, as drug problems are no different than other chronic diseases. Society must offer support and make sure that treatment is available for anyone who needs it. I hope that readers of Tales of Addiction will find comfort, especially if they have lost someone close to drug addiction."

—Joycelyn Woods, MA, CMA, Executive Director, NAMA
National Alliance for Medication Assisted Recovery

"Once in a blue moon, I read a book that culminates in poignancy by sharing a powerful experience. *Tales of Addiction and Inspiration for Recovery* is one such book: Here is a story and message amidst all of our stories; here is hope set against great challenges in the world of addiction and recovery; here is a legacy of understanding. *Tales of Addiction* is not just a collection of deep insight and personal accounts of tearful relapse and recovery; it is craftsmanship. Author Barbara Sinor is a well-read specialist in a world coming to grips with the disease of addiction. She offers her own valuable background of relatedness and heartened familiarity; artfully sharing all of this is the book's strength.

Like a tapestry, this book works by holding the reader's interest with unique tales smoothly interwoven with both a spiritual and intellectual thought process. Sinor progressively weaves the details of her life and practical wisdom in-and-out of the book's logical succession and its acumen of the disease of addiction. Some make it; others may not, you begin to know this. You feel your own relatedness and in the last chapters, the reader enters the author's space, hearing the breaking news of a sudden culmination of one very special story and a legacy that lives on in her. Sinor's book pushes forward with exigency and hope.

Tales of Addiction resonates a message to all impacted by the world of drugs and alcohol: It is a world of possibility and joy; it is a world of shocking sadness; it is a world of conquest. One poignant message from the book is that no matter what, a single addict's life is still sacred and knowing this captures a moment in time. Sinor invites the reader to share in her well of knowledge, reputation, and work in the field of addiction and recovery. She expresses touching wisdom gained from her own life experience while delivering generous individual contributions written by people like you and me. Tales of Addiction instills that there is no right or wrong; there is the possibility of helping just one more person; there is the possibility of coming to terms with this single moment, just for today."

—Bill Ford, *Addiction Recovery Blog*
Dad on Fire (www.DadOnFire.Net)

"In any healing process, the individual must first tell their story and become conscious of the core issues that precipitated their wounding. Once the story has been told, the work of healing and recovery can begin. Tales of Addiction provides this avenue for courageous story telling; one is struck both with the pain and suffering that was experienced, and also the hope for a healthier future. Dr. Sinor provides insight into the addiction process and the path to recovery pulling from behavioral theory, recovery philosophy, and the new understandings from the world of physics and spiritual development. Sinor provides a platform for those needing help on their journey to high level wellness."
—Leslie Lovejoy, PhD, Wellness Coach and Consultant, author,
Create Your Health Using the Five Keys to Wellness

"*Tales of Addiction* features an array of gut-wrenching yet heart-warming narratives by people with long-standing addiction issues. Weaving the unedited stories into a theme of empowerment and hope are Dr. Sinor's astute commentaries and observations. The stories are riveting, each starting out with family history that is inevitably pivotal to the storyteller's current situation. A must read for those with addiction issues and their families, *Tales of Addiction* is gripping because of its raw emotions and is effective precisely because of its variety and emotional power. It is a rare opportunity for helping professionals and lay people to perceive the common threads among all addictions, in the context of very compelling stories that make the lessons learned along the road to recovery memorable. Though suffering is a component of the stories, hope, insight and unconditional love are among some of the central ingredients to addicts' maneuvering the labyrinth of recovery while giving back to family, community, and themselves."
—Ellen DiNucci, MA, former Project Coordinator & Researcher
Complementary and Alternative Medicine Program,
Stanford University

Tales of Addiction

and Inspiration for Recovery

"These heart-wrenching and ultimately heartwarming stories, provide the inspiration for each one of us to know that recovery works."
Ken Seeley, PhD, host of *Intervention 911*, author, *Face It and Fix It*

Barbara Sinor, PhD

Foreword by Cardwell C. Nuckols, Ph.D.

From the Reflections of America Series

Modern History Press

Library of Congress Cataloging-in-Publication Data

Sinor, Barbara, 1945-
    Tales of addiction and inspiration for recovery : twenty true stories from the soul / Barbara Sinor ; foreword by Cardwell C. Nuckols.
        p. cm. -- (The reflections of America series)
    Includes bibliographical references and index.
    ISBN-13: 978-1-61599-038-2 (hbk. : alk. paper)
    ISBN-10: 1-61599-038-0 (hbk. : alk. paper)
    ISBN-13: 978-1-61599-037-5 (trade paper : alk. paper)
    ISBN-10: 1-61599-037-2 (trade paper : alk. paper)
    1.   Addicts--Rehabilitation--Case studies. 2.   Substance abuse--Treatment--Case studies. I. Title.
    HV4998.S565 2010
    362.29092'2--dc22
                                    2010009836

Distributed by New Leaf Distributing, Ingram Book Group, Bertram's Books (UK), Agapea (Spain) and other fine wholesalers.

Published by Modern History Press, an imprint of

Loving Healing Press, Inc.   info@LHpress.com
5145 Pontiac Trail   Tollfree 888-761-6268
Ann Arbor, MI 48105   Fax: 734-663-6861
www.LHPress.com

Contents

Acknowledgments

This book first started to manifest itself in a dream which took me by surprise, for I was smack in the middle of completing major edits of my earlier book which surrounds the field of addiction recovery. My office was engulfed in addiction-related materials in the same period of time when I was overwhelmed with my own son's addicted life. There was a longing to help guide both my son and his addicted friends to their sobriety—which I secretly knew was an impossibility, but I worked at it nonetheless. My dream declared that I was to write a book which contained other people's stories who were addicted or were on their recovery journey.

The dream also affirmed that the book was to be written to touch many readers, to help guide them toward compassion for those with a drug or alcohol addiction. I was given the title of the book, as well as a vision of its cover, just as I had received for prior books. It was clear that my instruction to write this book was a calling I was not to ignore.

As I collected each story, written from the contributor's soul, I knew my intention for the book was to portray each individual with honor, understanding, and nonjudgmental compassion. I began writing down information which came to me in sudden flashes of insight. I placed each story in a chapter to be read like the person was telling their potent tale out loud. I initially wrote with the intention of sharing my son's addiction story, with his permission, but not my own. However, as circumstances unfold within our reality, like they often do, it was clear that *my* story must also be included in the book.

I also dedicate *Tales of Addiction* to my beloved son, Richard. His life's journey resonates from the soul. I dedicate and honor all those who submitted their addiction stories; without their daring to share their pain and suffering, I could not have offered this important work to the public. In appreciation of their time and patience, I thank my husband, David; my sister, Paula; my daughter, Cindy; and, my superb publisher, Victor R. Volkman, for their support and patience as this book continued to unfold.

Foreword

Tales of Addiction and Inspiration for Recovery by Dr. Barbara Sinor is about the journey of the spirit. Born with the gift of God immanent (the Self or soul), the ego starts its development around the age of two. The brain is a marvelous receiver between the ages of two through ten, and it internalizes all of the hurtful acts and messages forming our basic beliefs about our self and our world. Maybe the most hurtful of all messages is what is *not* said, and what is *not* done.

When there is no one there to help you during the tough times and no one there to celebrate the victories of your young life, there exists a biological paradox as those who should be there for you become the sources of your pain. By the end of the teenage years, the ego has developed its distorted unconscious programs or scripts that depend on others to make our lives worthwhile. The one consistent occurrence is that these scripts are the source of great misery and suffering in our lives.

The painful part of life is not how painful each story is but how many painful stories there are in this world. This leads me to two very divergent notions. One goes like this... if we could end child abuse, we could substantially empty our prisons and our psychiatric units. Secondly—and most importantly—pain is a blessing for many as it confronts us with a spiritual opportunity.

What do I mean by spiritual opportunity? First, answer this question: Have you ever felt like all of your options were gone and there were no doors from which you could exit the pain of your existence? Have you ever felt overwhelmed? If so, the next question is: Do you think your ego or God was overwhelmed? Since you cannot overwhelm God, it must have been your ego. When the ego is overwhelmed, it creates a crack. It is this crack that allows the Holy Spirit to enter and for healing to start.

Throughout the stories within *Tales of Addiction*, it becomes quite easy to see how each person searched for *Something* to make their life easier, or to reduce their pain. This is the ego at work, instructing that happiness can only be found outside of ourselves. With this belief, we lose our God-given sense of joy and happiness of just "being in the moment." We spend our lives searching for the next great thing, or in this case, the next "high."

Alcohol and drugs are not the wrong direction—just the wrong method to search for our path. Alcohol and drugs many times give us a glimpse of the Self and our natural desire for transcendence. Desire exists when there is a sense of lack. If we do not feel a lack of something in our life, we would not desire anything outside of our self. In this manner, desire is a two-edged sword. The same energy that leads to alcohol and drugs could be sublimated into the opportunity to find a spiritual road to recovery. The human ego lives in the past and the future, and it is driven by fear. The power in *Tales of Addiction* is in the discovery that one can meet their fears head on. Guilt is always about the past, and fear is about the future which we can never predict. In spiritual terms, fear is an illusion—we *can* walk through it.

I gratefully thank Dr. Sinor for the opportunity to review her heartfelt work. *Tales of Addiction* is a gift from her Self to ours; it is her ability to see and understand the love and beauty inside of others that makes this book a source of healing.

Cardwell C. Nuckols, Ph.D.

Christmas, 2009

Introduction

Addicted or not, we all have stories to tell. Many recovering drug addicts and alcoholics are asked to write their *inventory story* while going through rehabilitation programs. These stories are sometimes called "drunk-alogs" or "drug-alogs." They try to share only to fumble with words that scratch paper like chalk on a board from years past. Sometimes words come easy, flowing like a river of grit and filth, covering the pages black. They see only words—words mixed with the flavor of a whiskey-sour or the last pin-drop of vodka settling in an empty bottle next to a slip of dust. Words of truth swirl downward into a spiral dance with unrecognized poetry left for judgment. With no glimmer of hope to stay straight and sober, inventory stories read like buttons on a shirt, repetitious and dry. Give a year or two of sobriety and these same words can declare emotions of hope, guilt, remorse, and pain; they become the true stories of an addict's life.

To begin writing an addiction story is like poking at the nerve of a hangnail—clipping it may begin a healing but you refrain because pain dictates your life. Each paragraph brings that pain to the surface to be held in awesome awareness as you realize you have lived the words on the pages. It is often suggested to those early *sobees* that it is "…important to reflect and learn *why* you chose to use or drink." Alas, such a shallow carrot to dangle! The newly sober have only empty words which spill over onto a blank page; but given six months or six years, these same words flow easily from mind to pen. They reach deep for shards of memories to fill their stories full of pitiful choices and past sagas of desperation and depression. Words then become a tool to unfolding the corners of life, revealing potent visions and rhythmic tales.

Addicted or not, we all have stories to tell. We tell how our skin crawls at the slightest scent of cigarette smoke or our aversions to kissing a drunk. We tell where our choices took us or how our life was lived without us. Whether stories from addicts or straight-chaired grannies, words keep us searching for truth and, in the end, guide us toward that *Something More.*

The stories you will read in this book are not from the well-known. They are not from celebrities you find in books written by another celebrity. You will not find names like Britney Spears, Robert Downey, Jr., Martin Sheen, Lindsay Lohan, Alec Baldwin, or other such people whose faces (insert 'frequently') we see but whose lives we know little about. The stories shared here are true, grit-bleeding tales told by people you will never meet but whose words will haunt you for months, or years maybe.

I collected the addiction stories in this book for two years. I advertised through a "Call for Stories" bulletin in several places including web sites, papers, journals, lectures, book signings, and workshops. I asked for stories to be submitted by those whose lives were touched by the effects of drug and/or alcohol addiction. The stories were to be personal tales whether submitted by those addicted, in recovery, or those whose lives are or had been affected by addiction in some manner. These stories have been edited sparingly.

Below is the advertisement which was released to solicit the addiction stories within this book:

A "Call for Stories" from Dr. Barbara Sinor

Therapist and Author: *An Inspirational Guide for the Recovering Soul,*
Gifts From the Child Within, and Addiction: What's Really Going On?

"I am currently collecting 'addiction stories' for my next book Tales of Addiction

If you have been or are addicted to a form of drug or alcohol, or you have been affected by someone who is or was addicted, and would like to anonymously share your story, please email me to receive online information on how your addiction story can be considered for inclusion in this informative book. Whether sober, using, straight, or in the process of recovery, everyone's personal story of struggling with an addiction can be a valuable insight for our younger generations, as well as an awakening call to ourselves as adults. I urge you to consider how sharing YOUR story of addiction might help both yourself and those facing similar life struggles."

* * *Email Your Story to: Barbara@DrSinor.com
In the Subject box, type "Addiction Story" to ensure receipt* * *
Or, write me: P.O. Box 382 Middletown, CA 95467

All those who submitted their stories returned a Contributor's Agreement which assured an acknowledgment in the publication of their stories with minimal editing and their choice of signature. It was also stated that there would be no remuneration given to those whose contributed stories were published. Woven together between these stories are excerpts, articles, inspirational quotes, and much of my own philosophy regarding addiction, spirituality, and life.

Chapters include stories from those who experienced difficult childhoods due to having a parent addicted to drugs or alcohol, and those who began their addiction in childhood. There are stories from those who have loved ones who are/were addicted to drugs and alcohol. Facts and information on recovery from addiction are presented throughout the book; also, inspirational material for recovery is included to guide those who wish to obtain help for themselves or others. Important literature, articles, and pertinent excerpts within the chapters bring a sense of hope and understanding. There are stories filled with pain and suffering, and those claiming hope and success. Lastly, each chapter contains inspirational quotes from well known teachers and spiritual leaders.

There are twenty addiction stories in this book, ranging from triumph over drug abuse to coping with the pitfalls of relapse and the challenges of recovery. Between the stories of those brave people who chose to submit their personal addiction tales, there is one story from my son Richard. His journal is interwoven throughout the book. My words which echo his pain and personal journey can also be found as my husband and I witness our son's life drama. His journey is long and reeks of stains of alcohol. Like many others written here, Richard's story is an incomplete play boasting glimpses of a warm, loving soul trying to fight the frost of alcoholism.

Barbara Sinor, Ph.D.
August 2009

1 *The Early Years*

When I was a little girl, about four or five years old, if I did something that upset my father, he would grab me by the arm and pull me down the hall where he kept the paddling board. As I remember, this board was an old ping-pong paddle. He would make me lower my shorts and proceed to give me three or four wallops from that paddle. It stung my bottom and made me cry, which I am sure was the intended result. One thing my father did not do was sit down and explain *why* I was getting the discipline which reddened my thighs.

I believe my father was treated much worse as a boy by his father who was a stern authoritarian schooled in the country hills of upper state New York. As I grew to discover my father later in my teen years and early twenties, I began to understand why, as an adult, he was unable to be the communicative, understanding Daddy I would have wanted as a child. He had been pushed and shoved into a life his younger-self found difficult to challenge and was thus unable to change it. This background left my father seeking a means to numb his feelings altogether; he chose alcohol.

With the help of the Re-Creation™ techniques, which I developed early in my career, I now can envision myself as a child and my father sitting side-by-side to hash through what was bothering him, or what I had done which triggered him to resort to the paddle. I have long since let go of any anger toward my father for his inappropriate behavior and have only loving memories left with which to savor our relationship. My son Richard's habits mirror my father's in some ways, not in others. I have imagined one or both of his alcoholic grandfathers (my father and my husband's), taking him aside and slipping him cigarettes and booze when he was a young teen. Maybe I can place blame on these two elder alcoholics for my son's addiction; sometimes, it is easier to look outside ourselves for the pain and guilt choking our hearts.

Humanity is on a fascinating journey. Each life impacts the next, expanding like a rainbow's arc through dimensions beyond our knowing. But, do any of us really know who we are or where we are going? I have heard the tale spoken by the late Reverend Billy Graham, addressing a large crowd when he was eighty-six-years young. It seems after wonderful things were said about him, Graham stepped to the rostrum, which overlooked an audience of thousands, and began his story:

> I am reminded today of Albert Einstein, the great physicist who, this month, has been honored by *Time Magazine* as the Man of the Century. Einstein was once traveling from Princeton on a train when the conductor came down the aisle, punching the tickets of every passenger. When he came to Einstein, Einstein reached in his vest pocket; he could not find his ticket, so he reached in his trouser pockets. It wasn't there, so he looked in his briefcase, but still could not find it. Then he looked in the seat beside him to no avail.
>
> The conductor said, "Dr. Einstein, I know who you are. We all know who you are. I'm sure you bought a ticket. Don't worry about it."
>
> Einstein nodded appreciatively.
>
> The conductor continued down the aisle, punching tickets. As he was ready to move to the next car, he turned around and saw the great physicist down on his hands and knees, looking under his seat for his ticket!
>
> The conductor rushed back and said reassuringly, "Dr. Einstein, Dr. Einstein, don't worry, I know who you are. No problem. You don't need a ticket even though I am sure you bought one."
>
> Einstein looked at him and said, "Young man, I too know who I am. What I don't know is where I am going."
>
> Reverend Graham continued his speech with a gesture, "See the suit I am wearing? It's a brand new suit. My wife, my children, and my grandchildren are telling me I've gotten a little slovenly in my old age. I used to be a bit more fastidious. So I went out and bought a new suit for this

occasion, as well as one more. You know what that occasion is? This is the suit in which I'll be buried. But when you hear I am dead, I don't want you to immediately remember the suit I am wearing. I want you to remember this:

I not only know who I am, I also know where I am going.

How fortunate Reverend Graham was in finding his way both on this earth and after! I can only pray my son, my husband, and myself do the same.

For anyone to discover where they are going, first they must look where they have been. After soliciting to the public to share their addiction stories, I was honored to receive dozens of letters and emails containing the life stories you will find within this book. You will read of lives filled with the burdens of guilt, anger, stress, disappointment, and regret which accompany the life of an addict and their loved ones. Also, you will read stories of success, transformation, and pride which paint vibrant pictures that capture all the passages of addiction and recovery. These first few stories are from adults whose childhoods were blackened by a parent's addiction, which tainted their life with sadness and pain.

*...the only way to tell some truths
is in the language of stories.*

—Richard Bach

A Small Child Called "Snivels"

It was a lively time again in Small Child's home. She giggled to herself and thought *Aunt Charlene's boobies are super big and funny! Why does she always show 'em to everybody like that?* Bellows of laughter roared through the tiny jovial house. The music was loud and daddy was singing along and dancing very funny with a big purple bottle in his hand. *Daddy is so silly.*

A comforting familiar smell of childhood, funny- smoke, wafted through the room where the children entertained themselves. Then crashing glass jarred Small Child from tranquility and, without thinking, she ran to see what had happened.

"Take it outside Bastards!" daddy yelled.

What's happening, I'm scared, Small Child thought. Standing in the middle of the living room, Uncle Bobby lumbered toward Small Child as he staggered; his white tee-shirt was covered in blood. Her eyes darted around only to find Uncle Fred in the doorway, holding a bloody knife.

"You're hurt Uncle Bobby; you're bleeding!" she yelled. *Is he going to die? I'm afraid.*

"It's his blood, Snivels, it's *his* blood, not mind!" daddy yelled at her.

Why is Uncle Fred so mean?

Daddy yelled at her again, "Get to your room and don't come out 'til I tell you!"

Daddy will take of care me, Small Child thought to herself.

* * *

The evening was dark with hardly any moonlight and its warm outside. His hands were on the wheel, but the car was bobbing back and forth between the lines like a ping-pong ball. She found the oddest comfort by staring through a hole in the makeshift door of the passenger seat. A rusted metal piece of a hole that was supposed to be there, where the door latch and window roller once were, there was no window now. *The black top moves so fast on the outside,* Small Child thought to herself. The yellow line was still weaving in and out.

"Youuuuu shhhure look lik your mmothner...Snivels," he slurred, looking at her, smiling with pride, and then turning the wheel along with his eyes and jerking back inside the line again.

I am beautiful. My daddy thinks I'm beautiful. She smiled back silently, thinking *I love my daddy.* Sensing his vulnerability, she seized the moment and asked yet again, "How did she die daddy?"

His smile faded as he stared ahead, wishing she had not asked. A burden, but with false strength and even determination, he blurted out, "She killed herself."

She heard the words again and again....and again in her mind, although he was not speaking. Small Child did not understand.

* * *

It was almost time for dance class. Small Child smiled while she put on her leotard and placed her tights on her toes to pull them up. Daddy bartered for her lessons by cleaning the windows of the dance studio. *I'm pretty,* she thought as she tied the shiny laces of her tiny black tap shoes, finishing the once-a-week ritual. Abruptly, her blithe mood halted when the voice of her father echoed to her ears. He was talking to the strange man that lived with us then. *Why is he living here? He is red-faced and smells funny.*

Leaving her bedroom, her sanctuary, she entered the living room and was disappointed to see both the stranger and her father with their heads hanging low and mumbling words, their eyelids heavy and droopy. *I hate the Greeny Meanies!* Oblivious to repercussions, she marched with fierce intention to the kitchen cabinet that held all the pills and took the bottle of green pills she so hated. She quickly hid them in her room to dispose of later, after the dance class. Never did she miss a dance class, ever. "When you start, you finish Snivels. I won't let you be a quitter like me." His lecture was simple and to the point. *My daddy loves me.*

Always disappointed that the time went by so fast when she was learning to dance, she saw her daddy's car just outside the window. *He's not smiling. Daddy is always nice here. What's the matter?*

His usual polite interaction with the instructor was rushed and they were out of the door in seconds. His jaw was set tightly; his eyes were menacing. *Stupid greeny meanies! He's always ugly on those pills.*

"I'm going to kill that muther fucker! He stole my greenies! After giving him a place to stay, he rips me off!"

The entire car ride home was a tirade of moral ethics. "There's nothing worse than a liar and a thief", daddy said so often.

"That muther fucker is going to die!" he repeated.

Having seen her daddy nearly kill a man before for less, she knew she needed to confess. *Otherwise, he will shoot him with his gun!*

Beginning to cry now, Small Child said, "No daddy, don't kill him. It's my fault. I hid the pills in my room."

With no hesitation or questions, he demanded she retrieve them; and then lectured her for an hour, ending the session with, "You almost cost that man his life."

Sadly, Small Child began to understand.

* * *

A preteen now in junior high school, the Child had a couple of friends who didn't seem to mind her used clothing and tattered appearance. One friend, Linda, whom she trusted implicitly, was going to spend the night. The young girl thought *I need to get the house clean before she comes over, and make it look nice, my first sleepover!* The friend arrived and the two girls retreated into the sanctuary. She was not embarrassed by her room; it was the nicest room in the house. Luckily, grandma bought her a beautiful queen-size canopy bed complete with butterfly sheets.

Evening was rolling in and the girls chatted over every subject important to junior high girls and listened to many records. Now bored, they decided to go outside. Plopping down on the grass under the tree, dusk was turning into night and their mischievous minds agreed on an old prank called "Ding, Dong, Ditch." They got the idea of *pranking* her own house, her own father. *Great idea!* they thought.

Without another thought, they acted, loudly banging on the door, then running to the backyard to hide, giggling and hardly able to keep themselves quiet. Suddenly, barreling out of the front door, like a crazed lunatic with hair mussed and a bit tipsy, came daddy, carrying his rifle! He fired a shot and screamed, "A man's home is his castle!"

The girls hid there, frozen, and watched while the police investigated her drunk father who pulled out pictures to show the officers his "darling baby daughter." *I hate his drinking. He's so sick. But I love my daddy, I just wish he didn't drink. I don't want to do this anymore. I have to get away from him.*

When the police finally left and the matter seemed settled, the friend said, "I'm going home."

[The following letter was written by Small Child, hiding in the eighteen-year-old's body. Her daddy was in prison; and she searched for inner peace.]

Dear Daddy,

Hey, hey, whad'ya know, a letter from your dear 'ole daughter! Miracles happen! How ya been? Me? Never been better! I'm working the 12-Steps in every area of my life and now my reality is a better place to be! I'm unlearning old patterns and re-creating my life. It works!

I work at Bob's Big Boy now and I'm paying back Grandma's money and saving for a car, a Fiero; a used one of course, but I want a Fiero and it's already mine; I just have to claim it. So, by the time you get out, I'd love to take the drive to come and pick you up! I may come visit you if I get it sooner. We'll see what happens.

You know I haven't seen you in a long time. I'm dying to meet you again! Now that you're clean and sober, I get to meet "you", not some crazy party animal legend, but good 'ole John S., father of mine. And you get to meet "me", not a rebellious fuck-the-world, let's party, crazy adolescent, but good 'ole Lynda S., daughter of yours. What an adventure this is gonna be!!

Grandma reads "Just for Today" everyday so far. She heals every time she reads it. With the both of us doing good for ourselves that helps heal her too. It's love. The better we get, the better she gets because then she's not a failure anymore. See what I mean? Guess I'm taking her inventory.

I think there's something you should know. You have raised a wonderful, beautiful, daughter who is successful! And do you know why? Because you are beautiful, wonderful, and successful today! That's the truth.

I was thinking about my childhood and upbringing. And it was awesome! It was very exciting, and sometimes dangerous. Perfect for me. Out of all the insane people and situations, I was taught how to survive. I can remember how you understood me when I needed a curling iron and bought me one. How you allowed me to go hang out with the black family down the street despite your own prejudices. How you allowed me to go to church with the neighbors and be baptized when you were an atheist. How you took me to the movies on my first date with a Filipino boy whom you were also prejudiced against. How you took me to dances with friends and when you took me to buy clothes.

No matter what crazy things we did and what happened, you *always* let *me be me*. As my only parent, you tried to understand. Nobody could have told me about my period and about sex better than you did! You are the best mother I could ever have! I want to thank you for the freedom of choice and belief you had in me, for allowing me to create myself. If I had to be born again and I could choose my parents, I'd choose you! You did it perfectly! As for the harsh words and violent moments we exchanged, they are forgiven. For myself and you, we make a great team when we're clean and sober. I love you, I really do.

Your Baby Girl, *Snivels*

— Lynda S.

"You gain strength, courage, and confidence by every experience in which you really stop to look fear in the face.

You are able to say to yourself, 'I have lived through this horror. I can take the next thing that comes along.'

You must do the things you think you cannot do."

—Eleanor Roosevelt

Saving Myself

I don't know when it started. It could have been that day, that week, that month; but one day I knew it. Something was different. My mother was an alcoholic.

I know that I was seventeen; that I was in denial; that I was lost. Everything was not all right. Everything was not safe.

When I was a young girl growing up, my home life was remarkably stable. I say 'remarkably' because there was always that underlying knowledge that my parents hated each other. When you're young, you don't always notice that your parents never hold hands, never kiss, never even just talk. And when they did talk, it was ugly.

My dad was never home. That was the one thing I did notice even when I was six or seven years old. He worked hard, he came home, he ate, he watched television, and then he went to bed and got up the next morning to do the same thing all over again. Nothing ever changed and that was what most of the arguments were born out of.

I never really knew my dad, even when he was home. Even now, I can hardly recall having had an actual conversation with him before the age of eighteen. We went on "daddy-daughter dates" to the local A&W, when I was thirteen, where he'd buy me a float and he'd talk about work as though I might understand the business of construction. I would rather have discussed my favorite show, my newly found passion for writing, or my renewed sense of faith after a youth trip to St. Paul, but I never said anything.

When I was finally old enough to view my parents' devastated marriage, I still held hope that things would change. Things only changed for the worse. One day, she did it. My mother filed for divorce, taking the step she knew he would never bother to take. She wanted to love someone again, to feel loved by someone else again.

From that day forward, things changed a lot. My mother grew out her hair, lost weight, and began to care for herself again. All those years I'd never noticed how beautiful my mother's eyes were. During my senior year, we became inseparable, best friends. It was the most amazing time of my life. I was making plans for school, a computer science degree. My high school graduation was magical despite my father's near absence. Everything was beginning to fall into place.

It was during this time that I'd noticed my mother starting to drink. First, it was just coolers and then wine and then beyond, and more of them. She'd wake up having forgotten the movie we'd watched the night before, and then she became a different person.

I'd gotten my first job and was adjusting. My mother started dating men who only seemed to aggravate her problem. I'd lay awake at night, waiting for the call in the middle of the night to come, and get her after a drunken argument with her boyfriend. I dreaded that phone, dreaded that drive but lived so much with the fear that if I didn't go and get her and something happened, or she was in an accident, I'd never forgive myself. So I drove, time after time.

Nights were the worst but the days were so opposite. She'd feel so sorry, want to change, and make so many promises that she'd truly meant at the moment but were quickly forgotten in the presence of an available drink. I remember all of the talks, all of the tears. She wasn't happy. This wasn't what she wanted but she just didn't possess the strength to change it.

I cried every night. I felt as though I'd lost all that I'd had and I couldn't keep the anger from slowly creeping in. First, I blamed my father; then I blamed God. Then I became so angry with my mother for letting this happen to her, for taking back everything she had taught me, and for helping me to lose myself in the process.

I began to believe that she couldn't possibly love me because someone who loved me wouldn't put me through this. In the most difficult of times, I turned to my writing and when we moved in with her boyfriend, because we had nowhere else to go, I started a website and a blog to reach out to others who were feeling exactly as I was and would understand and want to talk. My website and my writing became my salvation, as did my faith when I returned to it. I'd always known that there would come a day when I would have to choose for myself; I chose the Lord Jesus Christ. I'd grown up in the church and always believed so strongly but it was in the darkest of times that my faith became my own. I wasn't a whole person yet, far from it, but something was changing.

When I moved out and got my own apartment, I slowly began to rebuild my life to try and forgive but not to forget. To forget would be to let go of what had brought me this far. Though there were moments when I found myself at the lowest of points—moments of anger, sadness, grief, depression, and even moments where I felt as though I simply wanted to die—but now I've come to discover that I wouldn't take anything back. Nor would I want to relive any of it again.

At their worst, there were moments where I could hardly recognize my mother and the person she had become. There were nights of arguments turned into shouting matches—times when everything in sight was thrown against the wall and moments that turned dangerously physical. I felt so uprooted as we moved back and forth between her boyfriend and hotel rooms. But the most memorable feeling for me was the feeling of helplessness. I'd always been so independent and so strong but I found myself in a place that I didn't recognize with my mother, whom I barely knew, staring into a mirror reflecting a person I could no longer identify, and that scared me... it scared the hell out of me.

And then there came a day when I realized that as much as I desperately wanted to, I couldn't save my mother. That no matter how long I stood by her side, it was her decision and her decision alone. You can't save someone who isn't ready to be saved. I realized that as I was breathing the life that I could instill into my mother, I was slowly dying inside. I can still remember the day I first said this to my mother, "The only person looking out for me is me." And so I chose to save myself.

It's years later now and the healing is still ongoing, even as my mother has begun to accept and deal with her problem. I would be lying to say that I'm not still haunted by all that I saw and all that I went through, but now I understand why I went through it. I started a new website geared toward Children of Alcoholics this past year, as well as written more stories on the subject of alcoholism.

The darkest moments of my life sparked a passion in me that cannot be put out. One day, I want to devote my life to helping children of alcoholics to never have to feel the helplessness and loneliness that I did. Taking control of my life, I took back the girl, only to discover the woman I have become.

— Lacy M.

Just when the caterpillar thought the world was over,
it became a butterfly.

Zen Proverb

I have spoken many times about the relationship between childhood abuse and the use of drugs and alcohol. First, there is an unmistakable connection between those who have experienced physical, mental, sexual, and spiritual abuse as a child and their abuser being addicted to drugs or alcohol. Also, the correlation between those who were abused in childhood and the percentages of those individuals who become addicted to drugs and/or alcohol is high. The topic of child abuse has been in society's forefront for several decades and is becoming more easily discussed. Research estimates that one in three adult women and one in five men were sexually abused in their childhood.

My career has taken on a life of its own as my focus surrounding childhood abuse and trauma began to encompass the field of addiction recovery.

Gifts From the Child Within was the book to "break the silence" of my own childhood abuse. I realize how important it is to share childhood memories of trauma to at least one trusted friend or counselor. After the initial awakening to the fact that your childhood pain is real, there is a freedom which ensues with this acknowledgment and its sharing. The following submitted poem touches many of these levels:

Mister

There it goes again!
A noise I've heard before
I hear their feet shuffling, to her bedroom door.

There it goes again!
That noise I've heard before
I hear it every morning, around 3 a.m. or 4.

There it goes again!
I hear it clearly now
He emerges from her bedroom, sweat upon his brow.

There it goes again!
It's right outside my door
As I look downward, his feet are on my floor.

There it goes again!
I see urgent lust in his eyes
He puts his hands upon me, into my heart he pries.

There it goes again!
The pain I feel inside
Thinking about this person from whom I cannot hide.

There it goes again!
I look frantically through the door
I see my Mother by the couch, on the floor.

There it goes again!
She's holding a drink I've never tasted
I already know, she is totally wasted.

There it goes again!
My urge to cry out in pain
Knowing only too well, my cries will be in vain.

There it goes again!
My desire to comfort my sister
Why won't he leave us alone, this man my Mom calls Mister.
— Norma Jane

Not until we are lost
do we begin to find ourselves.
—Henry David Thoreau

The Best Minute of My Life

As a little girl, I loved my dad. And as our lives got worse, I would love him more. I felt that if I loved him enough, it would get better. My dad was an alcoholic and my mother was codependent. My parents believed in spanking with a belt or slapping us in the face as punishment. So it never seemed odd to me that they would hit each other. I thought they were punishing each other for being bad. Then the fights grew worse; later, I thought that they would kill each other when they fought. The neighbors understood too; when it got bad, they would take my brother and I in, sometimes late at night, even after we had already gone to bed. The next day, they would pack us up and walk us back home.

We moved a lot too. My dad was a good-looking man who had a gift for talking with people. Everyone liked my dad at first. When he got mad, everyone would apologize for him. Then they didn't want us around anymore; we would have to move again. My parents would tell me how it was all someone else's fault.

My dad would leave sometimes and be gone for long periods of time. Then we would get a call from someone to come get him. We would all go to where he was, sometimes to a bar to pick him up. He was abusive then to all around him. The people in the bar would yell at us to do something about him.

Sometimes, I would get to spend time with my dad while my mom worked. Dad would take me to bars where he would give me money to play the juke box, or get penny candy from the vending machines. The waitresses always liked my dad and would treat me nice, giving me pretzels or peanuts to eat. One day, my mom came home and my dad had a few friends over at our house. They were all drinking. He gave me beer too. Many times, his friends would get too friendly with me; no one ever said there was anything wrong with this. Not even my mom or my dad would say anything and they would be around, not always in the same room, but around.

My brother is two years younger than me. There was one night when I was in bed and I heard my parents arguing. We had to ask to get out of bed, so I called out that I needed to use the bathroom. My dad said, "That's it!" and went in and spanked my brother for talking while we were supposed to be in bed, asleep. I could tell the spanking was bad. My mother cried and said it was me who spoke; my dad would not listen. I just froze. When my parents came to check on me, I pretended to be asleep. My mother was angry with me that I did this, I could tell. My punishments from her grew worse; she now added being locked in my room for long periods of time to my being spanked. I learned to hold my need for going to the bathroom.

All this happened before they divorced. My parents divorced when I was five. After they divorced, my dad was through with us. We only heard from him on his birthday each year, when his family would pay for the long distance phone call. They were terrible phone calls. He would always be drunk and full of empty promises. He did not tell me where he was; only a new story each time of how happy he was now. With him out of our lives, my mother began her journey toward healing.

When I turned twenty-eight, I got a phone call on my birthday. I could tell my dad wasn't drunk this time and he apologized. He didn't even say what he was sorry for. I am actually grateful for that because I am able to put it toward anything I need. After that, we spoke weekly. That first call lasted maybe a minute. It was the best minute of my life! It was the start of my relationship with my dad. He didn't want anything from me except to talk to him on the phone. I didn't even know he was sick. He gave me closure with those calls. He helped me heal wounds that I didn't realize still needed healing. He said he was proud of me, allowing me to be the little girl who wanted his approval so much. I finally got it. I had told myself for so long I didn't need it, but it felt real good to get it. Five months later, I received a call from my aunt that my dad had died.

—Anonymous

2 The Turbulent Years

"Many of us think that happiness is not possible in the present moment. Most of us believe that there are a few more conditions that need to be met before we can be happy. This is why we are sucked into the future and are not capable of being present in the here and now.

This is why we step over many of the wonders of life. If we keep running away into the future, we cannot be in touch with the many wonders of life—we cannot be in the present moment where there is healing, transformation, and joy."

—Thich Nhat Hanh

So many of us live our lives asleep, not waking to the destinies before us. Einstein was portrayed within the story of the previous chapter as someone not knowing the destination of the train he was traveling on. Do I know where I am going? I do know where I will be when I no longer breathe. But, do I know where I am going today, tomorrow, next year? It seems to me that our entire lives are in *search-mode*. We search for who to be, where to go, and how to get there. If one of our greatest known physicists did not know where he was going while riding a train, perhaps it is not important for *us* to have all the answers to where we are going or who we are becoming.

There is an "authentic power" within each of us. I read that this actuality of authentic power "...happens when purpose aligns with personality to serve the greater good." Can you imagine a world in which everyone had authentic power? Author and therapist Marilyn Ferguson once said in an interview for the enlightening book *Towards A New World View,* "As we begin to see that each person has a heroic capacity, we discover that each of us has a destiny to fulfill." It is up to us individually to inquire, listen within, and discover where our private trains are headed. Some of us are in search-mode our entire lives striving to envision the tracks up ahead, instead of sitting back and enjoying the ride.

Most of us catch ourselves thinking, *someday I will get my act together,* only to resume the same patterns and behaviors which led us further down the street with a big hole in the middle. Ferguson continues, "If we want to get out of the mess that we're in, then we must realize that our old solutions to problems, our old worn ideas of how things ought to work are not going to get us there." These realizations can come in an instant, awakening our minds with freedom and opportunity. It is important to stay attuned to our greater ideals, to assume the victory that is waiting for us. However, it is not mandatory to realize all the details of the journey.

The diamond cannot be polished without friction
Nor the person perfected without trials.

Chinese proverb

Filling the Hole in My Chest

My name is Teresa ("Reesie") M. I am in recovery for drug addiction and for physical, sexual, and emotional abuse. I am an Adult Child of an Alcoholic. Let me give you a little bit of my history leading up to my recovery. My Mom was apparently quite a handful and came from a blended family with a large number of children. My grandfather, from what I understand, "gave" my mother to my father who was quite a number of years older than she was at the time. She was barely sixteen years old, and was married and expecting me, her first child. The relationship ended quickly and my mother married a Navy man shortly afterward. This would be the man who raised me and whom I considered to be my Daddy. My real father disappeared and I never knew him until later in my life.

My mother said I was an insatiable baby. I rejected her breast, was sickly, and almost died at one point. I was everything to her. Somehow, I think she believed that having a baby would provide her with enough love to fill the void she felt. It was something she spent a considerable part of her life seeking to fill; and daughter like mother, my Mother's mother searched all of her life.

We began life in a somewhat normal kind of family, whatever that is: me, my two siblings, my step-dad, and my Mom. My dad went to work every day and my Mom was a stay-at-home Mom. She kept the house clean, starched my Dad's shirts, and made three squares a day. I went to school with matching shoes to dresses and bows; we *looked* really good.

The first time my Dad hit my Mom in a drunken, jealous rage was when I was in the third grade. He sat us all down the next day and promised to never drink again. And he didn't drink; instead, for the next few years, our house became a pretty active place; people calling and coming by all the time and parties on the weekends. Dad dealt pot right in front of us. At the age of nine, my parents allowed me to smoke pot with them and I felt like a grownup. The very first time I tried it, I loved it. That's about when my father sat us all down and told us "What goes on in this house, stays in this house." So comes the first of many secrets, and the feeling that we were different.

My mother started drinking when I was about twelve years old.

She stopped coming home at nights and we didn't know where she was. My parents began to argue and fight almost every night. My siblings and I would sit in the closet, tearing at our hair and crying. I became my siblings' parents; getting them up and ready for school, making dinner, buying groceries, and babysitting them all day and all night. I also became the wife and mother. The fighting would be horrible, but in the morning, we would go about our business as if nothing had ever happened. This is where I got my motto for living: "Don't talk, don't trust, don't feel."

Finally, my parents divorced. I stayed with my Mom, who went full-blown into her alcoholic disease. Many homes were lost, many boyfriends came and went, and many times she would go out and not come home for days-on-end. I hated it. I learned that if I needed something done, I could only count on myself. I swore that I would *never ever* do that to my children.

Life was too crazy. My uncle came to rescue me one summer. He took me away on a fabulous vacation where he ended-up molesting me. My mother didn't believe my story, telling me that I dressed like a hooker anyway, and that I probably wanted it. So, at thirteen-years-old, I ran away with a hippy woman named Mickey and her daughter Dawn. We traveled all over the country and stayed with her family in Utah for a bit. Then she arranged to keep me in school in Santa Rosa, California. I ended that relationship by assaulting Mickey and going to Juvenile Hall. I was…angry.

I stayed in Juvenile Hall for about six months. My stepfather finally found me and brought me to his home in Healdsburg, California, to live with my other siblings and his girlfriend. My drug and alcohol use began here. My Dad informed me, "It's okay if you drink and party, just don't do it on the street where you can get caught. Do it here at home where you can share." I dabbled with diet pills, prescription drugs, pot, mushrooms, but mostly drank. I would sneak out of my bedroom windows and go to many parties. Because of my young age and my molestation, I was a bit promiscuous. My inability to stay in control while intoxicated cost me my virginity. ne night when I was out with a boy named Alan B., against my will, I went out to the car to vomit and he followed me. I could not fight him off; I was too drunk.

In high school, I remember a number of different scenarios. I quickly fit in as a *chola*, which is a female Mexican gang member. I starched my pants, wore low-rider attire, and even took on a Hispanic accent; I am Native American. Then I moved into popularity and became a cheerleader, drinking and partying after football games with the jocks who were a bunch of country boys. Eventually, I was chewing Copenhagen, wearing hiking boots, flannels, and a cowboy hat. I put down some beer, smoked some pot, and finally ended up in the 'smoking grounds', hanging out with rockers and going to concerts; then started using cocaine. It seemed I was a chameleon doing anything I had to do to fit in. I didn't place values on books and grades but on my looks instead, the guys on my arm, and where the next party was going to be.

My Dad became involved with illegal drug activity and our home and cars were seized after a drug raid. My Dad had to go "underground" for a number of years. He resurfaced a number of years later, strung out on heroin. Years later, he died as a result of this disease when I was twenty-nine. By age fifteen, I was basically homeless, sleeping on friends' couches and in cars. I lied about my age and got a job and a rented room of my own. Somehow, I graduated high school. I was all on my own and the "party" was on. I went from using a quarter gram of coke between six girls on a weekend to freebasing and eight-balls.

I did manage to get a decent job at a bank for a few years, all the while drinking and using, handing every pay check to my dealer. My relationships were abusive and dysfunctional. After almost losing my life to a cocaine overdose and a major beating from the boyfriend, a man who had been my customer from the bank intervened and took me to see a therapist; but I wasn't done yet. I would "call in sick" or ditch my sessions and eventually I ran-off with a much older man to another state, which abruptly ended my therapy. I thought that if I just moved away, I would have a fresh start and not have to use. Well, no matter where you go, there you are! So, I vowed never to use cocaine again…and I didn't.

My disease has been progressive. I would drink and drive, end up in places I didn't know how I got there, and then say I won't drink again; or, maybe just beer and wine. Then I would pick up right where I left off and do something stupid, swear off it, only to smoke pot. Then I would be fat and lethargic on the couch, depressed, and have to use speed to lose weight. So on and so on; each time I quit, I could not stay off it. I always ended up taking or using something. I always picked up where I left off and I was on a downward spiral each time, a little further down the rung.

I could always get a job, a house, a car, a boyfriend. I could always "look good" and get things but never keep them. I always ended back on the drug or the bottle; just couldn't quit to save my life! At one point, I had been living out of my car, panhandling a buck for a beer at the golf course so I could make dinner out of whatever they were serving for happy hour. Time and time again, I tried picking up and starting over, putting on my poker face and my big hair and big shoes to go to find another job, house, car, or boyfriend. *Then* I would be okay.

In 1989, I became pregnant with my first child and, as a result, married her father. Even though I was still drinking pretty heavily, I landed and maintained a job as a corporate executive. I had a nice house, a company car, my own staff and secretary, and an expense account. *But*, not even then could I stop using during my pregnancy. Instead, I limited my drinking and using to Fridays and Saturdays. It was, after all, my job to wine-an-dine my clients. Very soon after the baby came, I was back to using crank Wednesdays, Thursdays, and Fridays just to keep up at work and with the baby. I called in sick to work on Mondays, many times too hung-over or in withdrawals, unable to go to work. I am surprised they didn't can me!

Eventually, I was using alone and hiding it from my husband. I kept crank in my purse, in my drawer at work, and in my glove box. I couldn't even function without it, so I thought. My husband left me, my job was on the line, and I was fighting for the custody of my daughter. I was being accused of being a drug addict and an unfit mother.

Here's where the "bottom" hit for me. I had my daughter during the week but I wanted to go out one evening. So, I hired a sixteen-year-old babysitter and off I went. I ended up finding a guy on a motorcycle with a phat bag of crank, and well, five days later, I finally came home. The reality: I abandoned my child with a sixteen-year-old for five days with no phone calls, no diapers, and no food. I had actually done that "thing" that I said I would *never ever* do! I committed what we refer to as *incomprehensible demoralization*. I was so ashamed. I felt like a piece of crap. I wanted to die. That night, I lay in my bed unable to sleep and unable to forgive myself. I found myself asking God, "Why am I here? Is this all there is?"

I felt that people would be better off without me and I begged God to please give me one good reason not to just kill myself. It was about 2 a.m. Right at that moment, my daughter, just an infant, stood up in her crib and said "Mama." She was the reason! I began to cry. God Almighty had revealed himself to me in that moment, putting a magnifying glass on my life that I had a purpose and that He really did care about me.

I called my old therapist, Ellen. In our first meeting, she asked me, "Do you think any of the problems that you have in your life could come from drugs or alcohol?" I laughed. I called her a square. I thought everyone took something. It was as common as salt 'n pepper in my home. She said, "If it is not a problem, then quit." I did quit, but I couldn't stay quit; so she sent me to recovery meetings. I reluctantly went. The first meeting I went to, a woman shared that she had a giant hole in her chest that she was always trying to fill and that it was a God-sized hole and the only thing that could fill it was Him. She said she had been running around all her life trying to fix herself and fill that hole with drugs, alcohol, work, sex, and food. I realized then that I wasn't defective; I was an addict!

I began my recovery in 1991and by the grace of my Higher Power, whom I call Jesus Christ, I have been clean and sober for eighteen years. I have a new perspective on life. I have found joy and peace. I have since been married and we have a blended family of five children. My husband is a Pastor at an Assemblies of God Church. Together we attend meetings and have had the opportunity to frontier a program called Celebrate Recovery®, as well as attend NA and AA on a regular basis. I have a sponsor who has a sponsor and I work with women in recovery, sharing my experience, strength, and hope so that they can live a clean and sober lifestyle too. I read the books. I work the steps and I go to church. I have lived through the deaths of many close friends, my Dad, my step-dad, and my sister with her cancer, and I have not had to use. I can be a mom, a friend, a wife, a sister, a daughter and a gramma. My life is good today. I thank God and my program for a brand new life today. Thank you for letting me share.

— Teresa M.

The following two stories are the initial segments of mine and my son Richard's. Scattered throughout the book, you will find our stories intertwined like poison-ivy around the Calla Lilly. Our words spill from our souls as our paths widen yet overlap, as all mothers and sons demand.

My Story

As a child, my son always seemed lost. I have many pictures of him with his out-of-body smile hiding an old soul who wonders how it came to inhabit the little boy's body. Richie's young life was full of laughter and love. He experimented with all the boy-things like eating snails, peeing in the sandbox, and falling on his head all too often. His days were filled with the happiness of exploring his limits, and later testing those limits with his younger sister. Richie's life was typical for the 1970s until his father, David, and I divorced when he was twelve years old. I believe this childhood trauma exacerbated his feelings of insecurity which claimed his young life due to significant hearing loss and subsequent speech problems.

David and I continued a close relationship, exchanging the physical duties for our children every two weeks while living only a few miles from one another. This arrangement worked well for a few years. When Richie turned fourteen, I chose to move from the area. He was old enough to choose to stay with his father or move the five hundred miles north with his sister and I. He chose to remain in southern California to enter high school with his friends. This choice brought much confusion, guilt, anger, and frustration to Richard. I knew he felt abandoned by me. It is also the time period when he began what would become his life of alcohol abuse.

For the next eight or nine years, Rich and his sister took turns living with us both. David and I would meet at the halfway point between our homes in a small town called Avenal along a boring stretch of the five hundred miles between our families. Each time it was Richie's time to visit me, his talk became more detached, with little emotion or outward evidence of pain. He reported tales of school, good friends, and good jobs with his Dad. I tried to dig inside him to find the anger which clogged his heart but he did not allow me to enter. Thinking back on that time stings my soul with regret that we did not consider obtaining therapy for him. Perhaps then he could have learned to release the grip of pain his young heart clenched so tightly.

These years also teased Richie with success and freedom. He found a love of dirt bike racing which became an acceleration of risk-taking behavior. He commanded the rewards from both the sport and his father which was something he rarely achieved. Even though David and I were separated physically, it was never spiritually. Many times, I would join them on trips to the desert to watch and applaud Richard's daredevil display. Even back then, I silently questioned if he was self-medicating to abate his fearless behavior.

My Son Rich's Story

The first time I got drunk was when I was fourteen years old. My friend Robert and I got a six-pack of beer and we rode our dirt bikes up to the mountains at night, and drank. I remember vomiting and being sick. From that night on, we did this a lot and we started having fun together. More friends came along with us and this was the start of a ritual that lasted many years.

In these years, I started working for my Dad and others. The money I was making was more than any of my friends'; so after work, I could get my older friends to buy beer for me and I would get to go to their parties. I started to ditch school and was waking-up with hangovers, though I still made it to work just fine. I also started going to the local bar to play pool and smoke cigarettes. All of my friends did this, so I would always tag along. Peer pressure was why I started to drink beer and smoke cigarettes.

A couple of my friends and I started to drink hard liquor and liked it very much; even though I got sick, I kept on drinking it. We got into our parents' liquor cabinets and sneaked bottles outside all the time. I never had any problems getting alcohol.

Having money was *not* the reason why I drank a lot. My money was spent on material things such as my motorcycles and guns, all kinds of toys. I always placed alcohol last when it came to my wallet. But, when I needed money for beer, there was never a problem. Sometimes, I would spend all my money on beer, but I could and would replace it very fast.

Just being a part of a group of people was the most important thing to me. Even though I was doing *wrong* things, it didn't matter; it was all fun. I remember one day in my teen years, my friend Terry and I got drunk when his parents had a big company party at his house. We were drinking all day with everyone and we both got really sick. The next day, we both stayed home from school and didn't even go to work. There were all kinds of food and hard alcohol left over from his parents' party. So, we drank and ate all that we could. I remember drinking gin, vodka, bourbon, and many other types of alcohol. We were in the backyard when we heard the neighbors swimming, and that's when the biggest food fight ever started-up. We threw vegetables and fruit over the fence and they did the same thing. We emptied the refrigerator out! Then his Dad came home and there was food everywhere. We had to clean all of it up and got in a lot of trouble. All this started because we were drinking alcohol and got drunk.

When I went to school, I got teased a lot and had problems with my speech. But when I got buzzed, I didn't stutter and people didn't tease me. I felt that I was accepted and that made me feel good. I also hung around people that were older than me; even now, my friends are older. I felt comfortable around older people and they treated me differently than my friends from school. It was also very easy to get beer because they were over twenty-one! They would go to the store for me even if they didn't drink any beer. I never felt like I was being used by my older friends for my money because all of them had money and jobs too. But both age groups did influence me to go to parties and drink beer and hard alcohol.

I remember that I was accepted by everyone when I drank and I accepted everyone else. I never got into arguments or into fights; only with my Dad, occasionally. I became quite popular when I started to drink beer and smoke cigarettes. I didn't know that it was going to affect my schooling or my relationships with my family. I drifted away from them all and didn't even realize it. I drank beer just about every day as I remember, and never drank by myself, but always with at least one friend. I guess I was trying to get that feeling of being accepted.

I also had a lot of time by myself when I was growing up. My Mom and Dad had gotten a divorce when I was twelve years old. When I was fourteen, my sister went to northern California with my Mom. I stayed with my Dad. This gave me power to do whatever I wanted because my Dad was at work all day and went to bed early.

I could and would stay home from school and drink and party with my friends or work with my older friends and make money. Then after working, I would have one of them buy beer for me and go find my friends from school and get drunk at night; my Dad never knew. Even then, I would lie to get away with getting drunk. I lied to my Dad, my teachers, my family, and my bosses. I did all of this just so I would feel accepted. And now that I think about it, I did it also because I did not want to be alone; because I felt I had no family due to my parents being divorced.

You have to breakdown before you can breakthrough.
—Marilyn Ferguson

Learning to Walk Again

I would have to say the beginning of my life with alcoholism was while I was in my mother's womb. My dad abused my mom while she was pregnant and I was born prematurely as a result, weighing only four pounds. The story is that my dad was out somewhere, drinking, when my mom started labor and, having six previous children (their fathers had passed away; that's another story), her labor came quickly and my elder sister's boyfriend had to get her to the hospital. My sisters have told me that when I was just a little girl in diapers, my father once threw me down the stairs when he was drunk.

My first recollection of childhood has to be close to the age of three, that is, when my mom finally divorced my dad. My brother, who is eighteen months older than myself, and I were standing in a corner of the kitchen, watching my dad stabbing our mom. I remember trembling, crying, and being frightened as he stabbed her while we screamed. To this day, I get this churning in my stomach when I hear an ambulance. I remember them driving up to our porch and putting my mom on a gurney and taking her away.

Another time, my dad was driving while intoxicated (his choice of alcohol was beer, lots of beer) and was weaving back and forth, my brother and I frightened, standing behind the driver's side of the seat, not understanding at that age about alcohol; we thought he was just "having fun." He hit the sides of the cars parked along the street. My mom's door opened and she was dragged, I don't know how many yards, down the street, and he ran away so she would be blamed for the wreck. Next, I recall standing in the hospital, frightened, and they brought my mom by to see us because she wouldn't let them operate until she knew we were safe and sound. I remember looking up at her and seeing the blood and her face all torn up and bloody and being so scared. She ended up having stitches sewn on her chin from one ear to the other.

My mom was a pianist and worked a lot as my dad could never hold a job. He would go to a little convenience store or a pawn shop or wherever and hold them up with a gun to get money or food, and would end up in the Ohio State Penitentiary. It became the *norm* for us to have the police come knocking at the door and put him in handcuffs to take him away. I can't recall how I felt about this. I can only remember feeling numb, just watching him leave. My mom would take us to the penitentiary to see him through the window as he waved down to my brother and me. Again, numb, we would just wave back, with no feelings at all.

When my mom would be at a job, playing, dad would get drunk, walk up the stairs, and pick out one of his big leather belts from the back of our door (to this day, I don't know why those belts were there to begin with) and start beating and beating us as we screamed in pain. My brother and I shared one very large bedroom, he in one twin bed and I in the other. One evening, my brother came up with the idea, "The next time he comes up the stairs, throw the covers over your body and it won't hurt." Sure enough, it helped lessen the pain of that belt coming down onto my body over and over again.

I don't know what the mitigating factors were that my mom finally decided to divorce dad, but I don't ever remember missing him or even thinking about him. He was just gone. We didn't tell our mom about the abuse with the belt until years later when we were both adults. Understandably, it upset her. All I can remember during this time in my life is feeling numb, disconnected.

I know our lives changed when he was finally out. I remember having loads of fun with my mom like cooking and shopping. She would allow us to play "doctor" with her; we would stick toothpicks in her as if we were giving her shots and then we put Band-Aids™ all over her body. Such fun!

Then, when I was about four years old, she remarried a musician who also was an alcoholic (his choice was vodka, straight) but he hid it well. I can remember her taking us to his studio apartment and having chili. He seemed nice enough but I have to say, I didn't feel at ease with him. When he came to visit us at our house, he just didn't seem to know how to communicate with kids and wasn't a very warm person. I don't remember ever getting a hug from him or praise for anything I did.

They married. He was a lithographer and in the evenings, he would play saxophone, clarinet, and flute, when they had a gig. Sometimes he and my mom would play together in a group that they put together or she would play in one spot while he played in another.

We would be asleep upstairs when they would get home late at night. Apparently, he drank while playing and he would start on my mom when they got home. We would hear him through the walls and the heater registers in our bedroom, him screaming at her about how she "did too much" for us kids, or how we were spoiled, while none of the above was true. She was a truly good mother to us. She bought school clothes for us in the thrift shops; it wasn't like she was out buying all these elaborate items. Toys were few and far between but that was fine with us as we just enjoyed each other's company and played with our friends and enjoyed the outdoors.

But I can remember lying there, feeling badly for my mom and hurting, and feeling guilty just for existing. We both hated him for that. The next day, everything would be fine, just like nothing had happened. So many secrets. He, too, would wait for my mom to go to work and then he would start. He didn't beat us but he wasn't nice to us. We weren't allowed to speak at the dinner table. We weren't allowed to talk when we were going anywhere in the car; we certainly didn't laugh. Those younger years I don't remember a lot, but things escalated when we moved to the suburbs when I was about ten years old.

I can remember him drinking shots while practicing before he would go to a job. I still didn't put two and two together in understanding alcohol and his behavioral changes. When my mom would go to work, he would find some reason to mistreat either my brother or me, or both of us. When I was a teenager, I watched television commercials about different hygienic products. I can remember when a face-cleanser came out and some of my girlfriends were buying it and I wanted some. My neighbor gave me a jar of hers to try and I was so excited. I went into the bathroom and wet my face down, rubbed it into my skin, and waited for all the tingling and then, of course, washed it off in hot water. I have no idea how my step-dad knew how I washing my face, but he grabbed me by my hair when I came out and pulled me back into the bathroom, grabbing my wash cloth and screaming the whole time, "This is the way you wash your face!" He put soap on the cloth and scrubbed and scrubbed it on my face as hard as he could.

My step-dad brought a son into this marriage that was a lot older than my brother and me. We were so excited that we would have a big brother as our brothers and sisters were already grown and gone and had their own families. He was a loner, a great artist, but not a good brother. One day, he lured me into his bedroom by asking me if I would like to see some of his pictures. Of course, as a five-year-old that sounded great! Instead, he made me touch his penis and then he put me in his bed and raped me. I was so frightened and so ashamed. I was afraid to tell my mom as I didn't want to ruin her marriage.

This went on until I was approximately thirteen years old. During that time, I know I showed signs of a sexually abused little girl.

However, my mom didn't catch on. One day, I had gotten ready for school (first grade) and I just walked over to our couch and lay there, closing my eyes, not saying a word. He had raped me the night before. My older sister happened to be at our house, visiting. My mom called me to leave for school and I just lay there. This went on and on for quite a while until she got worried and told my sister they should call an ambulance. Knowing I was really okay—just raped—I opened my eyes. Nothing was ever said about it. It was my secret and I was ashamed and alone.

When I was about thirteen, I finally realized that I had the opportunity to stop him. When he came into my bedroom one night, I started screaming and kicking him and he never came into my room again. He joined the Navy and left.

I always felt different than everyone else in school. No one ever knew how I was being treated at home, not even my closest friends. I got pregnant my senior year, graduated, then moved in with my sister and her family, who lived on a farm in Maryland. After I had my little baby girl, I began dating. I guess as a result of living a childhood of abuse and my father's alcoholism my adult relationships were affected.

Repeatedly, I would date someone who was really nice, who was good for me and a good person in general, and accepted my baby. Then I would sabotage the relationship when I started to have feelings for the men. I actually was engaged once but when I got scared of my feelings, I left for Florida where my parents were living. I remember standing there in my mom's laundry room, talking to her about my plans, when my step-dad came home, saw me, and started screaming, "What is *she* doing here?" That just freaked me out. I stayed with my brother and his wife and got a job. I stayed away from my mom's home for a long, long time. I felt much anger towards my step-father. I hated him. He brought such hurt and disappointment and shame.

Later, my niece introduced me to a friend of hers that she had known for a long time. He seemed nice and it didn't seem to matter to him that I had a three-year-old daughter. We dated and eventually married, and then I became pregnant right away. I didn't even notice he was a beer drinker; I didn't pay attention. I never gave it a thought!

He started abusing me and coming home from work drunk, breaking and throwing things at me. When I was nine months pregnant, he came home late from work. I was in bed and I could hear him from the bedroom getting something out of the refrigerator. Then I could smell bacon cooking. All of a sudden, he grabbed me out of bed by the hair and started screaming at me about not having any bread in the house. At this point, I had no transportation and no phone, so there was no way I could go grocery shopping without him. He started beating me, breaking jars, and tearing up the house. He grabbed a butcher knife and came after me. I reached with my hands to stop him from stabbing me and held on with all of my might. At one point, he had the knife over my shoulder pointing at my neck and my arms were getting more and more tired. I was becoming too weak to hold it any longer. All I could do was scream. I saw a change in his facial expression and he let go of the knife; so I grabbed it from the floor and threw it out into the canal. I didn't have anywhere to go; so I was stuck in this relationship. My family didn't know what was going on in my home; I told no one.

I had my sweet little baby girl and everything was fine for a short while. Then one afternoon, he came home drunk. I had been nursing her. He started hitting me and grabbed her from my arms. He threw her across the room but thank God, she landed on the couch.

I guess my neighbors had to know what was going on in my home because they had to hear the screaming every time he would beat me. I had gotten to know a few girls in the neighborhood who were really sweet. This particular time when he came after me, I had gone outside, where I thought it would be safe, and he smacked me. One of the girls saw this happening and dialed 911. The police came and because it was his word against mine, they weren't going to do anything about it until she took them aside and told them that she had seen what he had done. The police asked her if she was eighteen years old and she told them yes, even though she was only fifteen. They handcuffed him and took him to Three Islands, a facility where they would keep him for 72 hours. I knew it would be to no avail to go to Legal Aid as I had tried that in the past. Even seeing the bruises on my face, they said they couldn't help me because it was his word against mine.

That's when my mom found out what was happening and I stayed with her for a few days. When he got out, my sister offered to have him stay with her and he started going to AA meetings with her as she too was an alcoholic but had not drunk for a few years. I prayed and prayed during those few days to know what to do as I knew I couldn't stay at my mom's house for long. He came to my mom's house after about four days and begged me to go home. He told me he would continue to go to his meetings. For the next four years, life was great. I eventually started to work at a local bank and we learned to live as a normal family, riding bikes and having dinner with my parents on Sunday.

Then he got involved with cocaine. He was gone for two days. When I got home from work one evening, I sat at the end of the bed where he was sleeping and told him he had a choice, the family or the drugs. He told me he wasn't going to give up the drugs, so I got an attorney and within three weeks, I was divorced.

Later, I happened to be sitting in my sister's restaurant when a gentleman came in that had known my family for a long time. He was a boat captain and a writer and was very interesting to talk with. Next thing, we started going out to dinner and taking my kids. I knew that he had been married before and had two grown kids of his own. He seemed nice and he drank rum and Coke™. Once again I didn't pay any attention to the alcohol, didn't think twice about it! He knew the situation that I was living in—having the girls, working two jobs, and still having financial problems. So, after about five months of dating, he moved us into his house.

He started drinking white wine at home by the gallon day after day. I would sit and talk to him and help him with poetry as he drank. I've never been much of a drinker of anything, maybe a glass of something once a month or less. He landed a job that he wanted as a project manager, overseeing the start of a new company selling yachts. He had been teaching me a lot about yachts as, at one point in his life, he had owned two of his own. He had always told me that he knew I had a high I.Q. and was quite certain that I could start my own marketing company and would do great working with him. So that's what I did.

I not only started my own marketing company but I started working for myself and made loads of money. I would give tours up and down the coastal area on a Chinese Junk. We were doing really well, but he continued to drink night after night. I had my girls moved to Michigan to stay with my sister and her family as I knew they would do well there. She was a good Christian and I loved her husband to death along with her two kids that were approximately the same age as my girls.

Then the abuse started. The more his job started to unwind and I was making more money than he was, he drank more and he started beating me. He would call me names and scream at me, and I would try to run from him, but he always caught up to me. I even ran outside one time for safety and I knew someone had to see what was happening, but nothing was ever done. Of course, he would say he was sorry and, of course, I would continue on.

Eventually, I gave up on my marketing company as I couldn't take it any longer, and we moved back. I worked for the Yacht Club as a waitress and became a hostess at my sister's restaurant. It was the most exciting day of my life when my sister and her husband brought my girls back home to me where they belonged. I had missed them so much!

Two weeks before Christmas, my husband was drunk and pushed me up against the wall and held a knife to my stomach, and told me that he could rip me open if he wanted to. I just stood there motionless, afraid that he would do just that. I had him evicted the next day. I was at least smart enough to put the townhouse in my name only. Here, I was back to square one with two jobs and not enough money to pay rent and utilities on my own. Back to getting anyone I could find that would share my place with me.

I met a really nice guy who was an Assistant Manager at a store that the girls and I frequented. Eventually, he asked me to go over to his house for a cook out and he was so funny and it had been so long since I had actually laughed, it was a welcomed change. We started having dinner together and I truly enjoyed myself. Then, six months later, we married. Here again, I chose someone who was a drinker and I didn't recognize it as a problem! His drink of choice was Black Russians. Then we started to have problems and I found out he was running around behind my back with other women. Instead of taking the girls and leaving him, I stayed. I don't know the answers to why I stayed other than that I loved him.

We went to North Carolina to visit my sister and it was so beautiful. I hadn't seen oak trees or smelled the earth for over twenty years; it was so refreshing. I convinced him to move to North Carolina to have a fresh start. He was an Engineer. We stayed in a little camper while looking for work. This was easy for me as I went through a temporary agency, but he was having trouble finding work right away, so he just continued to drink straight vodka day after day, and started being verbally abusive to me.

We eventually got our own place and we were both working. I was going to turn thirty-five and I wanted one more child, so I became pregnant but continued to work. The placenta separated when I was approximately six months pregnant and I had to have bed rest. My mom came up from Florida to help take care of me and to make sure the house was kept up and everyone was fed.

Well, I had been having some problems with my youngest daughter who at this time was about eleven years old, but I assumed it was because of the move and having to meet new friends. My other daughter was in high school and was approximately sixteen years old. One day she stayed home, not feeling well and my husband came home from lunch. He started screaming and carrying on about how her bedroom was a mess and just letting her have it. When he left for work, she made the comment that she hated him and I told her in a kind voice that maybe it was just because he wanted her to do things that needed to be done. Then she said something that was to change our lives. She said, "No, it's because he touches me." I sat up and asked her what she meant by that and she told me that at night he was coming into her room and touching her in her privates. I knew she was telling the truth.

Come to find out, he had been molesting her since we had moved to North Carolina, either at night when he would sneak in, or when I was trimming bushes outside. I was in shock. I called Social Services and they sent two detectives to talk with her. The only way that I would give them my name and address was if they would promise not to do anything until after I had my baby. I knew that I had to depend on his income since I had to stay in bed until the baby was born. I had to hold all of that information from him while still sleeping in the same bed night after tormenting night. I didn't want him to know that I knew what was going on. I had my other children stay in my daughter's bedroom to keep her protected.

He got ten years probation for what he did and my daughter had to move in with my sister in order for me to take care of my newborn baby. Then my plan was to get a job and get us out of there. But, I came down with Guillain-Barré Syndrome. I would fall and I couldn't get up, and my body was in so much pain that it was unbearable. At first, the doctors couldn't figure out what was wrong. First, they thought I had MS, and then Lou Gehrig's Disease, then lead poisoning or syphilis, but they were wrong. After six months of MRIs, morphine, eleven different antidepressants, tranquilizers, and anything to keep me from thinking clearly, they eventually found that I had Guillain-Barré.

It took me three years to be able to start walking again. Meanwhile, my daughter, who was molested, ended up having two children by him during my time with this disease because I could not help her. She allowed the first baby to stay with his other grandma, and then became pregnant again and allowed my brother and his wife to adopt the baby girl. She was only fifteen and sixteen years old and didn't know how to take care of babies, and I could not.

When I was well enough, I finally left him and did well on my own and now my youngest was approximately seven years old. I didn't trust my judgment in men any longer! I had a lot of anger towards him for what he did to me and what he did to my daughter. I knew because of what he had done to her, it would change her life as it did mine as a little girl. I blamed his alcoholism. I felt disappointment and disillusioned regarding relationships.

At this point in my life, I decided to get some counseling. I wanted to choose a good person in a relationship and someone who didn't have any drinking issues! My therapist gave me the okay to *not* accept a second date with someone that drank more than what I was comfortable with. I had this blind date set up by a good friend of mine and we went out to dinner. I watched as we ate and once he had that third drink, that was it. When he called to ask me out again, I told him that I really wasn't interested.

I started exercising a lot, power walking a lot, doing high-impact aerobics, day after day. When I would look in the mirror, I would see "fat" when, in reality, I was very skinny. I stopped eating very much but working out more and more until I finally had to seek help because I knew that I would die from not eating. Finally, I had the chance to get a job and do what I had to do. Then I met someone at work who would ask me out for lunch every day. He later told me it was a way to get me to eat.

We became good friends, I would go to his apartment and we would have pool parties and play volleyball. He would drink beer, but I would too. Not a lot as I have never really been a drinker, so I didn't think a lot about it. I figured it was because everyone was just having fun. After nine months of dating, we got married. He would drink maybe two beers in the evening after work; some nights, he wouldn't have anything. This went on for about five years, and then I noticed that he was drinking more and more. Now I was in another relationship with a husband who drank four to six beers a night, and during the weekend, up to twelve without thinking anything of it. His whole personality changed over time and then it was to the point where he was sleeping in another bedroom on a different floor of the house because I couldn't take the snoring and the smell of beer in his body. It really changed his personality. It made him more controlling and when he spoke; I never knew if he was telling the truth; and he was very self-serving. When we were having a cookout with my daughters and their husbands and kids, he drank a lot and then actually started flirting with my daughter.

As his drinking got worse, he started treating me like dirt in our office at work. He wouldn't follow through on the way I set things up to make my life a little easier. As he became more and more controlling, he wouldn't do anything I asked. It got harder and harder for me to deal with him in the office; however, I hung in there. Finally, he just told me he wanted to run the business, so I just let him take over.

Now, I am without work and I am finding it very hard to find other work. I am in a position of having to rely on him for everything, which I believe was his plan from the beginning. He knows I can't leave him (I have asked him for a divorce) without having a job. But, I will hang in there and keep trying.

Epilog: I have finished reading *Gifts From the Child Within* and it worked wonders for me. I now know that I am kind, good, strong, and smart; and my spirituality means a lot to me. I have been able to reach inside of me and find myself, and I am taking care of that little girl inside. I am now out of my depression and don't allow my husband's anger and control to determine how I feel each day when I wake up. I awake happy and I welcome anything that comes my way. Your book changed my life; from the very beginning, my life was being transformed. Finding the child within myself started me on the right path. I read every day and it enlightened my life. I now awake happy to be alive. I smell the air, and I feel light like a cloud.

I finally found a job after job-seeking for a year. It is at a church! I have people surrounding me that are great and it has changed my life. At a recent staff meeting, one of the men working there said he couldn't help but bring up the fact that when, "I walk into the room, it's like a light shinning." I thought that was the kindest compliment I have ever had.

I wake every day happy to be alive, truly enjoying my children, who are now thirty-seven, thirty-two, and twenty years old respectively. I also love my grandchildren too! I sit out back in my gazebo every evening after work and relax and enjoy all the foliage around me. I have you to thank and, of course, the Lord. Thank you once again for sending me your book which I have passed on to my daughter.

— Jeri L.

3 Recovery Hope for Loved Ones

Watch your thoughts, they become words, your words become actions, your actions become habits, your habits become character and your character becomes destiny.
—Frank Outlaw

The topic of recovery is one of the most talked about issues in society today. Recovery from addictions such as gambling, food, sex, and drug/alcohol abuse all share slots on our nightly television programs. Reality shows can be found which demonstrate people striving to shed their obesity, and those trying to rid themselves of drugs, prescription opiates, and alcohol. Recovery is not a new topic but recently has been made more widely viewable; this is a good thing. The public needs to see, hear, and feel the pain which accompanies the throes of recovery to believe it, to understand it. The topic of recovery opens our minds to the possibility of hope for ourselves and our loved ones.

Let's re-think recovery. Let's break recovery down; make it simple. It is easy to assume all the patterns we think of with the word *cover* in relation to addiction. These are some terms and behaviors we can associate with the word *cover*:

- **Run for cover**—running away from acknowledging addiction
- **Cover-up, hide, or conceal** our addictive behavior
- **Putting a lid on** our true Self, feelings, and desires
- **Going undercover**—not showing our authentic self

All the above actions have connotations of being secretive, negative, or dark. But, by adding two letters to the word "cover", making it *re-cover,* we find a positive set of instructions, giving us direction for self-recovery:

- We cannot *run* toward recovery but take only one step at a time, slowly discovering who we are without our addiction,

- We can break free from *hiding* behind fear, doubt, and anger, and move closer to re-covering our Self, our inner spiritual being,

- We can re-cover or *uncover* the pain and wounding which initiated our addiction,

- We can come out of *hiding* in our addiction-caves and learn to forgive ourselves and others, and

- We can re-evaluate and *re-cover* our dreams, goals, and desires for the future without our addiction.

If your search for recovery hinges upon the definitions in the first group above, move your view into the second group and form your thoughts into a more positive frame of reference. We must not merely cover up our emotions, our pain, our experiences, and our addictions. We must not hide them away, covering our woundedness in silence. We must not stifle our cries for help and direction. Instead, stand tall and voice your pain, disclose your addictions, and show your Self to others. Open yourself to those who are experiencing similar experiences and feelings. This type of sharing is what stories of addiction are based upon; by voicing your pain, your experiences, others may learn and grow.

According to an initial definition, developed by a panel of experts from the Betty Ford Institute, Recovery is "...a *voluntarily* maintained lifestyle characterized by sobriety, personal health, and citizenship." I like this definition because it sponsors the personal efforts of the addicted individual to voluntarily (accepting help and direction when needed) take those important first steps. Once in the initial phases of recovery, we have the opportunity to wake-up and search the many paths to our healing. We have the ability to learn and grow from our experiences and past digressions. Also, we can learn how to become all we were meant to be by helping others on their path to recovery.

Is it time for you to re-cover, to find and re-new your life, your joy? Is it time to re-cover your dreams from years ago and take your first step toward making them a reality? Recovery is a time to explore, learn, grow, and un-cover who you are. Many of those who have shared their addiction stories in this book were ready to take that initial step toward recovery by breaking the silence and reaching for guidance and support.

One of my favorite musicians is Josh Groban. Several of his songs bring tears to my eyes, even when he sings in languages I don't understand! When I am driving and listening to his CDs and he sings "You are Loved—Don't Give Up," I sing it loudly. I tell my son Richard to listen to the words, hoping he will understand how important it is that he not give up on his search for recovery.

> Don't give up
> It's just the weight of the world
> Everybody wants to be understood
> I can hear you
> Everybody wants to be loved
> I'll be there to find you.

"Every unexpected sorrow and pain—the death of a child or parent, a divorce or the dissolution of a relationship, the failure of a business, an accident or an illness—is an opportunity to grow spiritually. Even when a painful event happens to others, you can use your experience of it to observe and learn about yourself."

—Gary Zukav

Separately Forever

My husband and I were leading a happy married life even though we were living separately due to our jobs and business. We weren't having kids but still the life was happy. Then from 2006 onward, my husband was starting to lose interest in a sexual life. I thought this was due to business pressure or maybe he was in depression, but that our relationship was still okay. From July 2007 onward, he started drinking too much and started blaming me for every failure in his life. I am a well-settled woman in a government job, but I was also blamed for my job. It was a hell, but again I thought he was in depression and I could handle that.

On December 27th, 2007, his father died. All the relatives cursed my husband for not looking after his own father. His behavior became so different and unpredictable that I can't even explain it all. After a while, I came to know that he was having a relationship with a nineteen-year-old girl; quite probably, she was a prostitute.

Then he started using drugs excessively until we had to hospitalize him. We thought due to guilt and depression, he might have taken all the drugs. Life became a hell when he finally disclosed that he was addicted to drugs; he promised to quit. But actually he did not. He started stealing money from home and when we stopped giving him money, he sold our ornaments and jewelry. He started taking drugs in lonely places and I had to find him like a fool, and bring him home.

After that, I left him at his parents' place. They admitted him to an Ashram for three or four days. Everybody said that he was okay and he started talking with me on the phone saying he was sorry for what he did. After two months, we again were together. But after two or three days, I started doubting that he had quit the drugs. I tried to ask him and tried to convince him that he needed long-term treatment. But nobody listened to me.

The situation got worse and the old story of drugs began again.

He started blaming me for not having his child and the death of his father, and even for not correctly serving his parents. Again he started meeting this girl, taking drugs, and stealing money. Now we are living separately again. I have made up my mind to live separately forever. This is my sad story.

—Anonymous

There is no right or wrong choice.
The choice is irrelevant,
either pathway leads to your unfolding destiny.

Anonymous

Doing Nothing is Not An Option

My story is that of my daughter and grandson, who are struggling and looking to me for guidance and support, and as their mother and grandmother I don't know…how or what I should or shouldn't do. Most information I have read suggests that I use tough love which, to me, feels like I am turning my back on them. My daughter is forty-six years old and just recently, I learned that she has been using drugs since her teenage years. I suspected but never knew for sure. She hid it *very* well. I feel very stupid for not knowing. She was able to work her way through it and I think she is now drug-free. Or, am I still being stupid? She has always been very independent and has never asked for help.

On the other hand, my grandson, who was born when she was seventeen, is now twenty-eight years old and very dependent. He is constantly asking for help. I had no idea he was using drugs but couldn't understand how he kept losing his personal things; went from one job to the next; and has become paranoid, short tempered, and has a "victim" mentality. I now think that he could have been a drug baby. I did quite a bit of the care giving when he was a baby and noticed that he was not a calm baby; he cried a lot and woke up in the night a lot.

I love them both so dearly and it breaks my heart to watch them struggle. But I do not want to continue to be an enabler. Before I knew of my grandson's drug use, I helped him with his rent, food, and bus fare. I even sold my mother's sterling silver so I could help him. I pinched and saved so that I would have a few extra dollars to send him, thinking that as soon as he got on his feet, he would be okay. Then the confirmation came from his mother that he lost his jobs because he couldn't get up in the morning. This is where I drew the line in the sand. I wasn't able to verbally confront him so I wrote a letter to him saying I loved him but that I would not help him to continue his destructive behavior. He never acknowledged that he received my letter. But when he asks for help, he tells me he is "staying out of trouble." And also that he is starving, has no bus money to get to work, has no work, etc.

After we are done talking and I have said no, my depression sets in. My own flesh and blood is crying out for help and I can't help him. I have suggested he get into a 12-Step program; that he go to a shelter for food; and that he keep searching for work; but I don't see any effort. His mother tells him he can be a "functional addict" but that is not very helpful. I know this is a very common story so I would like to know what other people have done to keep their sanity. I certainly have not found the answer about what is helpful to do. As I re-read my story now, I can see that communication and tough love were too little and too late. Looking back can only bring guilt, regret, and depression. I choose to look at the here and now and try to find some new answers that will make a better future for all of us. Doing nothing is not an option.

— Helen P.

"To create a certain result, you must first learn to consciously align your thoughts, emotions, and beliefs with the desired outcome which will allow you to attract whatever is desired."

—James Van Praagh

How do we know when someone is *in* recovery? There are as many definitions of recovery as there are addicts. If we continue with the panel of experts from the Betty Ford Institute cited earlier, we find their definition in a section of *The Journal of Substance Abuse Treatment* (JSAT). This panel reports that personal health must be included as a component of recovery which entails not only the personal health of the individual addicted but also their social roles such as giving back to a community. Recovery then, "...may be the best word to summarize all the positive benefits to physical, mental, and social health that can happen when alcohol and other drug-dependent individuals get the help they need." (*JSAT*, October 2007)

Another valuable document, which relates the details of addiction recovery and effective treatment, can be found in The National Institute on Drug Abuse (NIDA) report titled *Principles of Drug Addiction Treatment: A Research Based Guide*, Second Edition 2009. This book states, among a list of informative data, that no single treatment is appropriate for everyone when it comes to guiding those addicted to drugs or alcohol toward recovery. Research dictates that treatment be readily available; address the needs of each individual including medical, psychological, social, vocational, and legal problems; and be of a duration that equals the severity of the addict. There is one item listed with which I take issue: Treatment does not need to be voluntary to be effective.

Even the best of intentions by family members, medical staff, professional interventionists or therapists cannot make the decision *for* an addict to seek recovery. This decision can only be made openly and honestly by the individual himself. We see all too often our loved-ones agreeing to "try" a recovery program, only to relapse soon after their release from its supervision. Also, within these thirteen principles of effective addiction treatment stated above, the spiritual component is not addressed. When so many of our known social abstinence programs affirm the presence of the religious or spiritual factor, how can the NIDA not recognize its importance?

My Story (continued)

While living in northern California during the 1980s, I was preoccupied with getting my Masters Degree and establishing my private practice. David and I continued to raise our kids "separately together." After eight years, we began seeing each other, dating again. Our children were young adults and they tested our rules, which actually threw us closer together; perhaps that was their unconscious plot! Soon David moved north to be with me which left Richard in our old house alone. Our daughter decided to move down south and tried living with Rich, but soon moved into her own apartment.

David and I remarried after a year's engagement. After another year of living in northern California, we also moved back down south into the house we had built together so many years earlier. This was a disaster. Trying to live with the old memories and emotions that were seeping from the walls of this old house launched a hefty challenge to our relationship. The only thing that saved my sanity was the promise of our moving into a new home where we could begin our second marriage without the history materializing from the first. This project took four long years to accomplish; Rich lived with us during this time of limbo.

It was easy for me to realize that my son drank each day; it was not easy for his father to comprehend this reality. David had a blind spot for his son. Many times, through these stressful years, I talked with Rich and tried to cajole him into admitting he was an alcoholic, not the thing to do. Of course he would not admit to being an alcoholic; he had no reason to do so since he didn't desire to quit drinking! Those four long years, I could only offer my tidbits of medical advice, an understanding ear, an appropriate kick-in-the-ass, and a mother's prayer that he not be put in jail when he received his first DUI. David and I began our long journey of becoming our son's enablers.

When we moved back to southern California, I kept busy writing and became the author of several books. I started a new counseling practice and received my Doctorate Degree. These years became a blur of text books, clients, writing, and trying to keep peace with my husband and son. David was the person to bail Rich out of the trouble he always *found* himself in. At this point, I noticed how Rich's drinking triggered my inner child and the memories I had of my father's alcoholism. Perhaps the same memory-dredging was happening to David too? Maybe, even our codependent behavior with our son was due partly to our being codependent children to our alcoholic fathers.

My memories of Rich's late twenties and early thirties are also a blur. Most of it consisted of his and my relationship flare-ups and his drunken rages, followed by our tears of forgiveness. I was living two lives, one as a forthright therapist directing others with their issues, and one as a mother shielding herself from her alcoholic son's violent tantrums. Another issue which unfolded due to Rich's drinking was how it affected my new marriage. With me around to criticize Rich's drinking behavior, David could no longer ignore it, and Rich was forced to admit it. Instead of my being a positive addition to their lives, I felt like an outsider who interrupted years of cohesive bliss. This, of course, resulted in a tear in the fabric of our relationship which took years to mend.

Soon Rich moved out and we lived minutes from him, which was much too convenient for him to pop-in to ask for money, food, rides, or help with medical and legal issues. When he was drinking, he would fume and rant, and even threaten us if he did not receive the answers he desired. We bailed him out of jail, helped with lawyers, legal papers, medical bills, social services, locating rehabilitation facilities, and all the other incidentals that accompany an alcoholic's lifestyle.

At one point, Richard agreed to attend family counseling with us. However, it was far short of what was needed to bring him back to long-term sobriety. He continued his alcoholic life as we watched in horror to what was happening to his body, mind, and spirit. Several times, Rich did voluntarily admit himself into residential rehabilitation facilities, but each time his sobriety lasted only about six months or less upon release. He finally acknowledged to himself, and the world, that he was indeed an alcoholic.

David and I were heart-broken that our son had chosen such a difficult path. We became more involved in his life and watched our own slip away. About this time, I was counseling a vibrant woman who wished to explore her motives for her life choices and soon I realized she was answering all her own questions, plus a few of mine! I suggested we end our professional relationship and just go have lunch together. This was the beginning of a long synergistic partnership with her supporting me regarding Rich, and I helping her sort out her life's direction.

Deborah and I thought we could solve the world's problems each time we met for lunch. Indeed, her sympathy for my situation with Rich along with her wry humor and blunt authority was just what I needed. Eventually, Deborah also became a counselor and we even collaborated on a book together. *Addiction: What's Really Going On? Inside a Heroin Treatment Program* presents her experiences while working in a methadone clinic.

Rich's Story (continued)

When I was eighteen, I was pretty much on my own and my sister was living up in the San Francisco Bay area with Mom. I was working full time in the union, laying tile and carpet. My Dad did the same work, so I was already experienced in the trade and was making a lot of money for my age. Even most of my older friends were not making as much as I was, I bought my first truck then. I had it all, even a new dirt bike. Now I could get beer by myself; I was even buying beer at certain stores; this was great. On the way home from work, I was buying a six-pack of beer and drinking it by myself. I now realize that this is when I started to drink alone.

When I got home from work, I would either go to a friend's house and we would go and drink, or drive to the foothills and go four-wheeling in my truck, or just drive around the neighborhood and stop by a friend's and drink. I and most of my friends had jobs and money, so we could go places and drink. Some disappeared or started selling drugs and did not drink alcohol. This group of people slowly left my life because they did not drink beer.

When I was twenty years old, I started buying whisky with my friend Robert. We both drank a lot of hard liquor together, and by ourselves. I was drinking more and more hard alcohol than I ever had, just about every day, buying half-gallons of bourbon and keeping it at home in my bar. Yes, I had my own bar in our house and my Dad never said anything about it. I was now drinking during work and getting in trouble. I did not realize what I was doing was so wrong; I drank by myself and in secret. This was very easily done because alcohol was legal and there were right and wrong times to get drunk in front of everyone. Then I was introduced to the bar scene.

An older friend of mine, Frank, was old enough to be my dad and was like one to me. He took me to a lot of bars and introduced me to a lot of people. Since I was a good pool player, this was a lot of fun for me, and I won lots of beer by winning the games I played. I got very comfortable in this atmosphere and made money from working to support it. Though I was going to bars every day and spending hundreds of dollars every week, along with a lot of my friends, I was having fun and was accepted to all who were in these bars. I got to be known well very quickly in the bars and had my own *tab*; this was great. Now I could drink alcohol even when I was broke! I thought that was so cool when I could take my friends to a bar and have a beer and tell the bartender to "put it on my tab."

Then my pay checks started to disappear faster and faster and I found myself driving drunk more and more from bar to bar. Eventually, I wrecked my truck and my friend Robert got hurt. I walked away. This should have happened much sooner and I am glad that I did not get a DUI then. By this time, most of my friends had wrecked their cars or had gotten DUIs, and this didn't stop me from my drinking habits.

I still had no real money problems or any problems getting my alcohol. When I worked and got paid "under the table", I was my own boss. So I could do whatever I wanted and this meant drinking on the job. I always had my ice chest full of beer and went to a bar for lunch; this was a must. This just became a habit, a daily routine; wherever I would go, my ice chest full of beer went with me. I was now drinking alone more and more. I was not drinking for social reasons anymore but to get a buzz. Maybe this was when I became an "alcoholic" and didn't even know it.

Then I started to miss work because of hangovers, and my paychecks were becoming smaller. It was a good thing that I had a tab at my local bar; it was the only bill I would always pay off every week. My other bills started to become late and real problems finally arrived in my life. My credit cards were taken away from me and I lost my second truck to the bank. But I still had money to get drunk.

In my early twenties, my Dad moved to northern California to get back with my Mom. My sister decided to move back into our family house with me. The both of us lived in the huge custom-built house, paying our Dad's mortgage, and shared the bills. I thought this was so cool. I had my bar full of liquor and a second refrigerator just for beer; even kegs fit into it. I could drink all the time and have parties whenever I wanted.

Football games were great on Sunday and Monday nights. My friends came over all the time to watch the games and get drunk. When I could, I would have women over, but at the same time, this was my sister's house too; she had started to go to college, and she stopped partying and got straightened up. My sister would get mad at me for having people over and disturbing her privacy. Also, the fact that I would just lay around and do nothing but drink beer all day and get drunk really pissed her off. But, I was still working and making good money. I could have done a lot more work; I was making just enough to pay bills and get drunk.

When I was about twenty-two years old, my sister moved out and got her own place. She was doing very well on her own and I stayed in the family house, and things got really bad for me. My drinking had gotten worse and my wallet got smaller every month. Now, I was only working for "under the table" money locally, just so I could pay my tabs at the bar and to buy alcohol. I found that working by myself, I could drink when I wanted to and show up on my time, and leave when I wanted. I did not have to answer to anyone. I started to live to drink. There was usually no food in the house, and I started borrowing money from my relatives just so I could buy food. I never paid them back. They all knew that I was drinking every day and ruining my life, but I would not listen to them when they tried to talk to me.

Eventually, bills were not getting paid, I just did not care. Even my rent money for my Dad stopped and I was borrowing more money from him to keep the gas, electricity, and telephone on. But, I still made enough money to pay for alcohol. During this time, I started to drink hard liquor by myself. I liked it because all of my problems went away and I didn't feel hurt or alone. I hated these years of my life; I felt unwanted but knew no one really left me on purpose.

4 Hitting Rock Bottom

"It is not the absence of the fear but the courage to take action anyways that determines success. When we learn to face our fears, we learn to observe our thoughts and feelings but not be ruled by them. Instead, we choose how to shape the lives we want."

The Daily OM

Whether recovering from childhood trauma, the effects of current world affairs, alcohol or drug abuse, or the loss of a loved one, we are covertly supporting one another. We tend to forget just how important we are to each other and that we have an impact on those around us. The truth that all people are connected has been written about by many scholars and spiritual leaders throughout the world—*all souls are connected*. If you are on your own journey toward recovery, you can be assured that there are millions of others ahead of and following you.

Spiritualist Eckhart Tolle instructs:

"You can always enter the Now from wherever you are." What this tells us is that we have the choice to begin healing at any time. We always have the power of choice to start on a new road or to continue on the path we have long trodden. Our journey though recovery from whatever drug, behavior, or trauma can be a clear active step toward creating the life we have dreamed. However, this path requires our direct choice to move forward. If the butterfly does nothing to start the motion of flying, it stays earthbound in its cocoon; and when it does flit its wings, it is felt around the world. *Action incites results.*"

Here is an excerpt from my book *An Inspirational Guide for the Recovering Soul* which may motivate you or someone you love to make that first choice:

> In the early 1980s, one of the people I found myself admiring was actor and author Shirley MacLaine. Her book *Out On A Limb* was one of my favorite readings, which I faithfully devoured, then recommended to all my friends. Looking back on that period in my life, I now realize why Shirley was such an inspiration to me. It was her willingness to act. She was and is one of those courageous people who actually take the steps that pave the way for others. Her need to explore her inner Self and share her findings, gave millions the "go-ahead" to dive into their own journeys within. I was one of those who learned that without action, there is no actuality. MacLaine writes in *Dancing In The Light*, "Everything we feel, think, and act upon is interrelated with everything everyone else feels, thinks, and acts upon. We are all participating in the dance."

> *It is time for you to dance your dance...*

There always seems to be a sense of resistance when a choice-point needs to be made. We intuit a need for growth, for change, but somehow feel held back by fear and doubt. Spiritual teacher and best-selling author Debbie Ford states, "Resisting our present reality will not bring us any closer to our desired reality. In fact, resistance is the glue that keeps us stuck in the very circumstances we most want to change." If you are currently reading these words, perhaps it is time for you to choose an action to take you one step closer to who you are. Ford continues to tell us to "surrender our resistance" and allow a natural flow to unfold:

> Surrender requires us to give up our attachment to how we think our lives should look. It means we have to give up our need to control the situation and resign as General Manager of the Universe. And ironically, as soon as we no longer need things to be different, they begin to show up differently. Surrendering our resistance is like opening a door to another level of consciousness where serenity and ease reside.

Challenge yourself to find one gift, one talent, that you have been resisting to manifest. This first action might even lead you toward the path of recovery, if this is desired. Imagine that merely making one choice toward creating something unique for yourself, could lead you on a silent path of inward reflection and allow the spirit of the Universe to emerge from your soul to help you take that initial step.

As children, most of us played the game of making shadow figures on the wall. We would sit in a darken room with a bright light focused on the wall and hold our hands in different positions trying to come up with the best animal shadow-figure. Spiritual entity Emmanuel asks, when we look at the shadows on the wall, do we believe this to be reality? Or, are we also aware of how the shadows were created, and of the brilliant Light that remains behind them? He instructs:

> Not only are you the shadow
> that is dancing on the wall,
> But you are the hand
> that makes the shadow,
> and you are the
> Light.

The next several addiction stories were written by those whose struggles took them to their "rock bottom," but they found the strength to emerge from their darkest night and walked into the Light once again. These stories reflect the impact each of us has on our relationships and our connection with reality. I honor their life struggle and their stories of soul transformation so others might benefit.

As human beings, our greatness lies not so much in being able to remake the world... as in being able to remake ourselves.

—Mahatma Gandhi

Methadone for Life

I am a sixty-year-old woman and have been on methadone maintenance treatment since 1969. That's right, more than forty years.

My husband, Peter, and I both grew up in suburban Essex County in New Jersey, enjoyed happy childhoods, and both became intravenous heroin users. Pete began using heroin first and I was horrified when I first saw him injecting himself. However, after a while, I also began using heroin. I stayed home alone or I took up the game.

After several imprisonments and other problems associated with drug addiction, we decided that was not a viable lifestyle. We had two small children and wanted better, not only for them, but for us as well. A friend of ours steered us to a doctor who was prescribing methadone and that medication became instrumental in affording us the opportunity to live more normal lives.

We both became gainfully employed, purchased a home, and basically lived the American dream. We successfully raised four children, were active in local scouting groups, and served in PTA organizations and other groups.

In the beginning of our methadone maintenance treatment (MMT), we were given a prescription by a local doctor for a week's worth of methadone at a time and had it filled at a pharmacy. As MMT became more widespread, the government put tighter restrictions on methadone. It could only be prescribed and dispensed at specially licensed clinics.

My husband and I pretended that taking our methadone was similar to someone taking insulin. We needed it every day. We didn't feel it when we took it, but we certainly felt it if we missed our dose. If methadone is used correctly, it can change your life.

After a few years, the methadone tablets we had been taking were replaced by the biscuits and then by the methadone in a liquid form. Some clinics had the clear methadone mixed with water and others had the thick red syrupy mixture. We found that the methadone seemed to work best for us when taken with a hot beverage.

We had our good days and a lot of bad days. We talked ourselves through it by taking it one day at a time. Each evening, we would say, "Well, one more day under our belts."

One tool we used was to list *goals*. Every time we achieved a goal, we checked it off. When you are able to see in black and white that progress is being made, you can feel good about yourself.

Pete and I were competitive and we used that as a tool also. Each of us would think that if the other could do it, then so can I. Neither of us wanted to be the quitter.

During the early days of MMT, and in some areas today, neighborhoods didn't want methadone clinics nearby. All drug addicts were envisioned as vicious criminals. My clinic had a group of us go to several community meetings to address them.

We convinced them that a drug addict can be anyone including their teachers, firemen, policemen, lawyers, etc. It was difficult getting certificates of need for MMT clinics because local communities didn't even want to admit that they had drug problems.

My personal opinion is that some people in MMT are not taking full responsibility for their sobriety. Responsibility is a big word and encompasses a lot. There is responsibility for admitting you have a problem, responsibility for taking steps to correct, and responsibility for staying with your decision for sobriety.

Some clinics, through public and funding, will arrange to get you to the clinic, medicate you, counsel you, and deliver you back home to your door, all courtesy of the government. I feel this is wrong. After all, you didn't need to be taken by the hand before to buy your drugs and the government certainly wasn't paying for it. So why do you need it now?

Everyone is different. What helps one may not help another, and some people do need more help than others. However, sometimes things matter most to us when they are earned through hard work. Is it easy? No!

However, most things worthwhile are not gotten easily. If you want something like sobriety badly enough, it is definitely worth the work. Unfortunately, too many patients use methadone on top of other drugs and that works against their recovery.

A lot of drug addicts need to rebuild the trust of their families and friends. This cannot be done overnight—just as trust wasn't lost overnight. We all need to take the small steps necessary to show our families that we're staying on the road to recovery. Pete and I always felt blessed in recovery. Our daughter thinks she had the best parents and life ever. Evidently, we were good actors! We also have three sons and three grandchildren.

When our children were young, we only told them what was necessary at the time. Generally, we said we were getting medicine at a clinic. As they got older and asked more questions, we told them that we took bad drugs many years ago and now we're taking medicine to help us keep from ever doing that again. We didn't want to lie to them. We always thought that once a child catches you in a lie, you lose your credibility. As they became adults, we told our children the whole story.

I remember hearing for years about "getting high on life" and I used to snicker at that—I don't anymore.

It is nice to have your family together and being proud of yourself, instead of being the "odd man out." Life truly is wonderful. It is a lot more fun being healthy, owning a home, going on nice vacations, and being financially solvent than living day to day on drugs.

— Sandy L.

"There are many paths that lead to liberation or enlightenment. No one path is the 'right one' or 'wrong one.' However, there is one requirement: You must practice and apply the principles of your chosen path with consistency and determination."

—Richard A. Singer

Finding A Path That Fits

I awoke in a dark, gloomy, dungeon-like hotel room in northern Florida, trying to figure out how my life had gotten so out of control. I hadn't changed or showered in a few days and I felt like all my humanity had been suddenly sucked out of me. I consisted of one endless void that seemed impossible to fill. I abruptly realized what had happened as I rolled over and had no idea who was lying next to me. Once again, I relapsed and spent close to two thousand dollars on cocaine; for what reason, I'm not sure. In the past thirteen rehabs, they told me I had a disease but my mind didn't want to believe this. As a young man, I could control this malady they called addiction; I could save myself. I believed I was all powerful and all knowing. I was an omnipotent being that didn't need the help of anyone.

Well on this day, something was different. I was beat up, jobless, penniless, and I had just called my mother for help, and she said she wanted nothing to do with me. This was her way of helping me to realize that I needed help desperately. My heart sank and I contemplated suicide once again. At this point, I had two options available to me; either, surrender to this disease like it was being suggested by the treatment professionals and begin recovery, or end my life. Fortunately, I chose recovery and began my path toward growth and a quality of life that I could never imagine.

Early recovery was difficult; however, I was determined to stay sober a day at a time and make something of my life. With the help of addiction professionals who were genuine, caring, empathetic, and real, I was able to make progress on a daily basis. I trusted them and this is what made recovery possible. I didn't know what I wanted to do but I did know that I wanted to stay sober and those around me helped in every possible way they could.

Throughout the growth process of recovery, I was urged by my Higher Power and I chose to enter the field of addictions to help guide others to the life that I was given through the miraculous process of recovery. I ended up going back to school and accomplishing great feats that I could never have imagined. I graduated with my undergraduate degree and pursued my Master's degree in clinical psychology. During those years, I continued to work in the field of addictions and was mentored by incredible individuals in this field. I was taught to work with passion and care, and to advocate for clients no matter what.

I have grown since the day I stepped into recovery. I have been blessed with a gift to be a therapist that cares about one thing only: helping clients improve their lives a day at a time. This thing, which many call "work," is my life. Therapy and helping others enjoy a better quality of living is my life and I continue to be blessed on a daily basis with clients who want the help to get better. Little do they know that they help me more than I could ever help them. They give me strength to keep going on a daily basis and they share with me their personal lives and world. This is truly a gift.

I've come from the depths of insanity, from sleeping on the street to working with individuals much like myself, who want to live a better life. The best part of it is that my new position, which I recently accepted, is in the Cayman Islands. Who would have thought that an alcoholic and addict could have an advanced degree in psychology and be helping others better their lives, and in a tropical paradise! It's not something I would have ever imagined eight years ago when I entered recovery. Life for me is all about helping others, which is the one pertinent key for the evolution of humanity and the universe. Never, never, never, ever give up on a human being! It took me many tries, but eventually I succeeded.

— Richard S.

Richard's book can be found in the Bibliography

If you want something you've never had before, you need to do something you've never done before.

—Anonymous

Being The Lost Woman

I'm addicted to anything I do more than twice and what makes me feel good! My life then immediately becomes out-of-control and unmanageable. I become obsessed with trying to feed the insatiable "hole in my soul" with anything and everything, and almost always toxic. Please note, I stated "trying" to feed; I've never succeeded in feeling satisfied while in active addiction.

I am a woman in my late forties and have been battling my addiction to alcohol and drugs since 1987. I found the 12-Step fellowship and was able to maintain sobriety for seven years until in 1994, when I was given the shocking information that I was *the family secret*. I found out that the man who brought me up, the one I called Dad, wasn't my biological father. Evidently, in 1958 my mother had a love affair with another man who was a friend of the family, my non-biological father's best friend. This information rocked my world. It answered a lot of questions that I've always had such as, why didn't I look at all like my two older sisters or why I never felt loved or even liked by the man who brought me up. I resemble my biological father and I reminded my dad of who I really was, or more importantly, who I was not, and the reality of the painful betrayal caused by my mother.

I wish I could say that I was able to accept this with all of the spiritual grace of a woman rather than the morbid grief of a child; but I fell apart. My entire identity and life was a lie. I wasn't the Italian American Princess my tee shirt said I was. I was the Polish illegitimate bastard child who was never going to be anyone's "Daddy's little girl." In my very Italian household, I grew up hearing a lot of negative jokes about non-Italian people. If I used drugs in the past to numb any shame or feelings of being a defective reject, then I was off and running before long. The month I found out who and where my biological father was, he died of lung cancer. They buried him just four weeks before and I would never meet him. His widow wanted nothing to do with me and denied knowing anything about me.

The man I was married to for a little more than a year was very Italian and very disappointed that his new bride in recovery wasn't worthy. The small, selfish man couldn't handle the fact that I wasn't the Italian thoroughbred he was promised; he left me. He couldn't very well take his Polish wife to the "Little Sons and Daughters of Italy" meetings and socials!

Shortly after that, I became involved with the man I'm married to today. Although he was new to recovery in which I had remained clean and sober to this point, he didn't judge me. He didn't care about what my breeding stock was or was not, and rather than feel the deep pain of abandonment, I immediately replaced that pain and became involved with this new man. We married six years later and have been together seventeen years.

When I first met my new husband, I knew he was relatively new to recovery. I had just celebrated my seven years in sobriety but had emotionally and spiritually stopped growing after learning the truth of my identity, and I succumbed to the sweet relief of depression. I was introduced to heroin and began inhaling what I thought was the answer to every problem and believed I'd soon have the solution to world hunger. Little did I know within months, my own children would be the victim to a world of poverty of their own because of my new best friend, heroin.

Imagine the denial. Snorting heroin, throwing up, and then feeling the most incredible peace and self acceptance that I'd ever come close to feeling. This denial and promised progression eventually brought me to becoming an I.V. drug user. Broken promises to myself: "I'll never use heroin. "I'll never put a needle in my arm." "I'll never mainline cocaine." "I'll never put any drug use in front of my kids." "I'll never share needles." Oh, the denial of this powerful disease!

I began using heroin when I was thirty-six years old. If you think it can never happen to you, or if you believe you're above it, exempt from it, or too old to try it, you're lying to yourself. I was brought to my knees by this drug faster than anything I've ever been addicted to in my life. I used black tar heroin and began having seizures from the neurological trauma and damage, falling out and flopping around in public, sometimes two and three times a day; still, I continued to use. I've had my utilities shut off, accompanied by several evictions, in and out of detox centers, had multiple overdoses, and couldn't even feed my kids a can of string beans... still I used.

Looking back, I just have to believe I had a loving Higher Power in my life protecting me from the throes and dangers of addiction. I became a pathetic, lost woman. I had burned every bridge in terms of family and friends; the community I lived in saw me as a deviant threat. I was also denied help in every detox/rehab facility because I had signed myself out against medical advice time and time again. At this point in my life, I just accepted that this would be my destiny. I saw no way out and I made several attempts at taking my own life, only to be awakened violently from the familiar doses of Narcan or charcoal and stomach-pumping, which the paramedics or trauma team would administer to me.

Coming home one day, my sixteen-year-old son greeted me at the door and said, "Mom, sit down, we need to talk." I cannot even describe the courage my son had to muster in order to risk what he was about to say to me. I thank God for this brave child. He laid into me, an intervention that ultimately saved my life. He told me he could not sit by and watch me slowly kill myself; it wasn't fair to him. He was only sixteen and he was embarrassed to bring his friends home. There was never anything to eat and he always went hungry. His clothes were never washed; the landlord was screaming at him for all the back rent I owed; and he couldn't even take a warm shower because our hot water had been disconnected. He told me seeing the inside of my arms made him sick; they were always bruised, bloodied, or infected. He told me he loved me but if I didn't get help by the end of the day, he was calling the department of Child Foster Care so he could live in a safe, warm, foster home, where people weren't strung out and at least pretended to care about him until he was an adult. "Mom, you need help," was what he told me.

It was at that point when I realized that as long as I knew he still loved me, there wasn't a mountain I couldn't move. The next morning, I made an appointment with the inner city methadone clinic for an intake. I couldn't find a detox facility to admit me because I didn't have insurance and I had a reputation for leaving Against Medical Advice (AMA), so I chose the methadone clinic. I knew I was ready; my son loved me! It took a couple of weeks of appointments, physicals, in-depth interviews, and sixty dollars to begin, but I did it. My husband joined me. There is no way in a relationship that one partner can get and remain clean and sober without the other one working at it as well.

That was eight years ago and although I had a couple of one time relapses, I immediately came back and have remained alcohol and drug free for almost four years. I believe that when my son stepped up and loved me out loud, I had a reason to live. I may have started recovery for him, but today I am here for me. Both of my sons are my heroes for never giving up on me, loving me when I was so very unlovable and so very sick. I was sick physically but I was also sick spiritually. I had one heck of an emotional hemorrhage bleeding uncontrollably in my soul until I finally surrendered.

I was a chronic *relapser* for years until I was graced with an amazing woman who has been working with me at the methadone clinic where I am receiving treatment. She was working with me for free with the basis that I give everything I have to getting well; now she believes she has done all she can. It is the only medication that has seemed to offer me hope, in addition to the weekly therapy and outside 12-Step meetings.

I believe methadone is a powerful form of treatment, as long as the addict utilizes this medication as a temporary tool of their recovery process, not a permanent way of life. It won't successfully work without the commitment to hard and honest work towards self-healing. I believe methadone is often misused as a quick fix or band-aid therapy and unless the addict excavates deep inside their soul, unless they work the steps by searching for that spiritual hemorrhage that has kept them in self-destructive bondage, relapse is inevitable. I've witnessed too many addicts trying to feel a "buzz" from this medication and who are being over-medicated to avoid the temporary discomfort of the process of self-inventory. I also believe this is why the treatment of methadone is often judged as a negative and controversial medication. I am presently on 31 milligrams of methadone; I was on 90 mgs. I am working with my counselor to safely taper and eventually detox completely to live a methadone-free life.

I am also working on my issues behind the diagnosis of Post Traumatic Stress Disorder (PTSD). I grew up in a horrific physically, sexually, and emotionally abusive relationship with my family, whom I am detached from, but who still are in my life today. I often feel re-traumatized because of their inability to seek recovery and because they are active in their disease. I struggle with not wanting to live a victimized but rather victorious life.

I think if I was to try and help another addict seeking recovery while telling my story, I would have to tell them truthfully that it's not as easy as some people claim. I've heard, "Just pick up and go to a meeting." It is true, however, coming into recovery from a life of ripping and roaring as I did—and most addicts do—not everyone, who knows you, are willing to "embrace the new you." No one wanted anything to do with me; I couldn't be trusted. They had all heard the "I'm going to get help" line one too many times. I was still needing a place to live; I was unemployable; I owed everyone money, and I was in debt up to my ears. I even struggled in the 12-Step fellowships in my area because I've been through the revolving door there for years. So, getting clean and sober isn't always so black-and-white. I was still feeling very crispy from poor health; I lacked confidence, and I felt very shame-filled, defective, broken, and forgotten by God.

Sometimes being the lost woman, indeed, felt more comfortable in terms of familiarity. I knew how to run. I knew little more than the trouble I was facing and the excruciating pain I was feeling. I was tired. I found a counselor in the outpatient treatment facility I was attending, who saw something in me that I didn't see in myself. I would listen in his groups and I would share. I would humble myself and ask the group for prayer. I would watch the women who were working, going to meetings, doing things with their families again; they had a spirit of integrity and joy. I saw some serious and profound changes in them each week. I would pump them for guidance, whatever I could. I put everything I had in trying not to fail. The cravings were sometimes intense, but my desire to rebuild was stronger. The message I heard was this: "If you want something you've never had before, you need to do something you've never done before" and "If you always do what you always did, you'll always get what you always got." So the bottom line was "change"; if nothing changes, nothing changes. Wow! What a concept—complete radical and spiritual change. My life hasn't been the same since I truly accepted this. I'm still changing.

One of the biggest changes was allowing someone healthy into my life as a mentor, recovery life coach, not instead of but in addition to the suggested 12-Step sponsor. When my counselor, whom I trusted, presented a particular woman to me, I was ready. I believe that my Higher Power purposely and intentionally hand-picked this woman of grace for me. We started slowly; she asked me, "Who are you? What do you want?" I really didn't know but I knew just staying clean and sober wasn't enough for me anymore. I had to peel the layers of years of abuse, shame, and whatever wounded me so deeply that I was willing to self-sabotage myself. I knew the drugs were only a symptom of something much deeper and I knew I couldn't possibly begin this journey alone. I gave her what little I had at the time to work with. I cried; I sobbed; I became honest, vulnerable, and raw. I told this woman a few things that I had done and what had happened to me, things I swore I would take to the grave. I purged every

Wednesday morning at 7:30 a.m.; for almost four years I showed up.

Today, when someone asks me who Kat is, I tell them, "I'm still learning." But I have learned what being true to myself is. I certainly have had several experiences which cost me dearly just to learn what being true to myself really meant. I've learned my likes and dislikes; I have formed opinions; and I have found my passion for creating. I have been blessed with several God-given talents that I've nurtured and have turned into a part time business. I sew and paint primitive folk art dolls and I go to flea markets and tag sales. I take old cheap or thrown away junk and strip, clean, stain, distress, repaint, and embellish these items to make them marketable again. I turn trash into treasures, the same way God did with me. I meet wonderful people at local craft fairs where I sell my work. I want to begin teaching women in recovery how to make "spirit dolls" or "inner child" dolls to help themselves begin to nurture and lovingly take care of themselves. This will help to remind ourselves that we need to do the same thing with our inner children who reside in our own souls.

I have a voice today. I'm still struggling with so many issues now that my energy isn't spent trying to stay clean and sober the way I did in early recovery.

These are the two best gifts in my recovery: Having a choice and having a voice! I lost my non-biological dad three weeks ago, the same week my eighty-two-year-old Mom was diagnosed with inoperable lung cancer. But, I am not missing in action; I am right here for her, for my family, for God to use me when He needs to. I won't ever return to the caterpillar that I was before changing into the beautiful butterfly I am today. My war is over... I am free!

— Kat

5   *Creating Reality*

Our thoughts direct everything in life. Think of thought as the conductor of our life's symphony.
—James Van Praagh

Most people today have accepted the fact that we—our thoughts, our actions, and our reactions—help shape our reality. This metaphysical principle is being considered more thoroughly by the frontiers of science where it has already been established that an observer's presence actually appears to change what is being observed. Now the notion of "backward causation in time" involving human intentionality is being suggested in scientific research.

Can the present affect the past? Can our thoughts create our future? Can we re-create our thoughts? Our emotions? Our lives?

The process of Re-Creation™ found in *Gifts From The Child Within: Self-discovery and Self-recovery Through Re-Creation Therapy* testifies to these questions with an astounding, "Yes!" The research in the above field contends that observation and intention in the *present* can influence events in the *past*. Research by Helmut Schmidt, renowned German researcher who instigated retro-psychokinetic elements, shows us that an observer's present intention appears to *change an event* that happened in the past, therefore, backward causation in time. Further research by physicist Henry Stapp has been conducted which takes human consciousness into account in this field, not just material used in a laboratory. Stapp has presented a theoretical breakthrough of a nonlinear standard to quantum mechanical equations. (Schlitz, Marilyn. "A Question of Evidence" *Noetic Sciences Review*, No. 34, 1995.)

What does all this mean to you or your loved one surrounding healing or recovery from addiction? Consider the theory of relativity which states: All events are happening at once, there is no space or time. Our future, our present, and our past are all happening at once. I know this is a big theory to swallow, but read on. If we visit our past, held in our subconscious mind, our memory mind where memories are stored, we can revisit the traumatic incidences and the negative experiences we have undergone. Then, we can literally and consciously re-form or re-create those memories into a more positive event, a more positive outcome. We can in essence re-create our past by transforming our emotions, our feelings which are attached to those memories. Our thoughts can also be re-created to more positive visions based on these new emotions and new scripts.

With these more positive thoughts, we now can let go of some of the negativity surrounding our past traumas and begin to make positive present and future choices and decisions. Ultimately, we move forward with more positive thoughts of our past, and thus, create our present and future reality within a different frame of reference. We have the ability to transform our past pain which may have been the *cause* to our *effect* of our addiction.

As noted in quantum theory, thoughts are matter—thoughts are things which even create our emotions; those emotions are also creating our reality. We can take those positive thoughts and emotions into consideration consciously, as well as subconsciously, with the intention to create our present and our future from a place of healing and recovery. *Belief precedes experience.*

Yes, the present can have an effect on the past. Yes, our thoughts can create our future. Yes, we can re-create our thoughts, our emotions, and our lives. This can be done without expensive therapy. You can begin re-creating your past experiences and negative emotions to help release subsequent addictions. The following addiction story was written by a man who realized he could develop his own "re-creation techniques" while he was trying desperately to undo his muddled past.

My Drug Addicted Life and Recovery

From grammar school through high school, teachers periodically made comments on my grade reports such as, "John is a capable student but he will not apply himself." They were right. I did just enough to get to the next grade. My dad wouldn't let me quit. Because I was seventeen during my entire senior year, I needed parental consent. Though I wasn't enthusiastic academically, my father still managed to instill a value for education that would surface in my life almost thirty years later.

My lack of academic initiative was exacerbated by the ethos of the 1950s. The influences of rock-and-roll and James Dean were spurring out a breed of rebels that would turn into the hippies and druggies of the 1960s. So it was with me. In 1956, when I was eleven years old, upon entering junior high school, I started drinking on weekends. Unlike youngsters of later generations, I didn't start experimenting with drugs until the summer of my high school graduation in 1962. I certainly would have, if it had been offered to me. In a nutshell, I went to a party when I was eleven years old and didn't get back until I was forty-five. Over a period of more than thirty years, there was scarcely a time when I wasn't on the lam, doing time, paying fines or restitution, doing community service, serving probation or parole, pending court, or suffering the loss of my driver's license. I considered those repercussions *dues* that I had to pay to continue to live the way I wanted to.

My parents were awesome. Being their only child, I pretty much got whatever I wanted and did whatever I wanted to do. They were not strict disciplinarians, though I did spend my share of time on parental restriction. Nor was I abused in any way; therefore, I don't blame them for my drug and alcohol use. I got high to have fun. Having fun was my goal in life and I avoided responsibility like it was a germ.

By the end of my 15th summer in 1960, I was an alcoholic. I landed in jail three times within a six-month period. Each time, I had been drinking. My first night in jail was for curfew. Probably the most significant thing about my first arrest was meeting a new friend who remains one of my best friends today. Jim and I had one hell of a good time in that jail cell: climbing around on the bars like monkeys, tearing up the mattresses for cotton ball fights, and yelling obscenities at the cops. From that point on, going to jail wasn't much of a threat.

A week later, another friend and I were busted for petty theft, stealing milk off someone's porch because our mouths were dry from drinking wine all night. Eight months later, I got my first drunk driving ticket on my Cushman Eagle motor scooter. My driver's license was revoked before I was eligible to get it. I was jailed again the night after graduation in 1962 for trespassing and again later that year for stealing hubcaps. There were five more charges in 1963 for minor offenses, two of which got me sixty days in the county jail.

Once when I was incarcerated at the Glen Helen Rehabilitation Center near the county jail in San Bernardino, California, two of my friends joined me there. We played practical jokes on each other, met new drug connections, and planned what we were going to do when we got out. It was not an unpleasant experience. Not only was being jailed for the night not much of a threat, serving time wasn't either. After I was released, one of my friends asked, "Well, how did you like it?"

I smiled and said, "I liked it." Compared to what I was expecting, I did like it. To me, it was like being in a boys summer camp.

I was a happy kid, a happy-go-lucky teenager, and later, a *relatively* happy drug addict. So why did I quit? Because my life was going nowhere; my family was concerned about me; and I knew my mind and body wouldn't take the abuse much longer. So, after more than thirty years of drug and alcohol addiction, I quit. It was a process, however, rather than simply a decision.

Would I change anything if I had it to do over again? No! Why not? Because I wouldn't be who I am today if my life had been lived differently. In my opinion, happiness is part of a temperament that is innate. Of course, life circumstances can alter that, but I believe that the basic temperament is static. If trauma doesn't strike and we have had a stable and loving foundation in early childhood, most of us are capable of handling most of life's encumbrances. That's my opinion, anyway. However, I don't believe I could have remained very happy if I had not stopped. Trauma—physical, mental, or spiritual—would have inevitably struck in some form or another.

Before I elaborate anymore on my shadow side, I should comment on the shining star in my life, my daughter Lynda. We lost her mother when she was four years old, so before and after and between wives, I raised her. She gives me a Mother's Day card every year. She and I agree that my drug and alcohol addiction during her childhood has not damaged her. She inevitably became an addict herself, however, but she found recovery after only five years of drug and alcohol abuse. She got clean and sober before I did and then she hoped and prayed that I would also find recovery. Today, Lynda and I are best friends and she has brought two more shining stars into my life.

Fortunately, my two grandkids will never have to see me the way my daughter did. They'll never have to watch the police take me out of the house in handcuffs, like my daughter did. They'll never have to control their behavior according to what drug I was taking, like my daughter did. And they'll never have to endure being embarrassed in public, like my daughter did. The most important thing that I can share today is that it hasn't been necessary for me to take a drink or put a needle in my arm since May 7, 1990 (my last relapse date), and for that I am eternally grateful.

I have been arrested over forty times for various misdemeanor and felony offenses, served five county jail sentences, many probations, and a three year state prison sentence. Fortunately, I was released from parole early for collegiate scholarship and compulsive attendance in 12-Step meetings. Since then, I have become responsible and accountable for my actions, which I wasn't previously capable of.

Addicts have an automatic denial system, especially when it comes to their addiction or when they've been accused of something. Before I went to prison, my querulous old friend Jack called me on the phone to explain, or whine (most drug addicts are chronic whiners) about being arrested for a burglary he didn't commit. He carried on for five minutes about the injustice of it all. The whole time he was ranting, I thought about the thousands of burglaries he had gotten away with. Finally, I asked, "Jack, why are you so outraged about this?"

"Johnny, I didn't do it! God damn them! The bastards are trying to frame me," he insisted.

I calmly replied, "What about all those burglaries you got away with over the last twenty-five years, Jack?"

"What? Don't get carried away Johnny. The fact is I didn't do it. This charge doesn't have anything to do with what I did before," he dismissed my question as ridiculous.

While I was in the county jail, I overheard the following conversation, "Ya know Frenchy, I wouldn't be here for rob'in that liquor store if the damn clutch wasn't bad in that old Chevy of mine. Just as I was taking off, the motor died. I got it started, then it died again. That happened three times. By the time I made it to the corner, there were red lights everywhere."

"I hear ya bro, if my old lady's mother wouldn't have turned me in, I wouldn't be here either," replied Straight Razor.

I could identify with those middle-aged bikers because I have all too often placed the blame for my behavior outside of me. It would have been a waste of time to say, "Frenchy, you wouldn't be here for rob'in a liquor store if you hadn't been rob'in a liquor store." It's strange, but that obvious statement is absurd to them. So it was with me at the time.

While having a beer on my night off in the bar where I was a bartender, one of our regular customers asked if I could get him a quarter gram of speed. I said no. Later he asked again. Again I said no. However, when he asked me again around one o'clock in the morning, I knew that there was some in the bar, so I got the drugs for him. He was an undercover policeman. I fought the sales charge in a jury trial and lost. I took it all the way through the court of appeals and lost that too. *I was entrapped. It was not my fault. They were picking on me.* The truth is: If I had not sold drugs, I would not have gone to prison for selling drugs. However, like Jack and those bikers, I was incapable of being accountable for my actions.

I was forty-three years old before I made it to state prison. I had been knocking on the door for twenty years however. As the judge looked at my rap sheet, he said, "I can't figure out why you haven't been sent to prison before!" Then he looked at me and said, "I can't believe that I'm sitting here trying to talk myself out of sending you to prison now."

My rap sheet didn't have violent crime on it. Though there are couple of burglary charges and a robbery charge, they were investigation charges that didn't result in conviction; in fact, they didn't get past the arraignment or preliminary hearing stage. Most of my offenses were drug and/or alcohol related. I believe that's why judges were hesitant to send me to prison. But by the time this judge viewed my rap sheet, there were forty charges that took up several pages. As it turned out, I am glad he sent me to prison.

A few months after I arrived on the prison yard, there was an experimental program starting called Project Change. It was a nine-week education and therapy program designed for pre-release inmates. On the flyer was a request for interview. I knew that I would never terminate parole successfully unless I refrained from the use of drugs and alcohol, so I filled out the request form and interviewed for a place in the program. I only wanted to remain abstinent for as long as my parole lasted; then I planned on returning to what I was before

I was incarcerated, a fun-loving, dope-fiend, party animal.

While tending bar prior to going to prison, two of my friends used to come in and drink soda. "What's up with this, Jerry?" I asked.

"I'm on parole. If I don't give my PO (parole officer) any dirty tests or have any brushes with the law, I'll get off parole early." Jerry and Lisa both got off parole thirteen months after their releases; so I was determined to do the same.

I was accepted into Project Change six months prior to my release date. Since the program was just starting, they needed to fill the dorm that was allocated for the program. Later, only inmates in their last sixty days were eligible. A month later, I got a clerical position with Project Change. Never having used a computer, I found an inmate in the education department who tutored me until I was familiar with the word processing program on Apple computers. Once I was proficient, I typed questionnaires, work sheets, and other classroom material, much of it gleaned from Hazelden recovery books. We held classes five days a week in the TV room and part of the dorm was also converted for other classroom activities.

Another reason I volunteered for the program was for the fringe benefits. Project Change students would go to chow first and they would be first in line for commissary, linen, as well as, mail call. I am surprised that more inmates didn't volunteer, if for no other reason than the fringe benefits.

Even prior to my enrollment in Project Change, the letters I was receiving from Lynda, my then twenty-one-year-old daughter, were motivational and rife with 12-Step clichés and jargon. She seemed genuinely happy in sobriety. I was not much of a father to my daughter and even less of a son to my mother. I had caused them more anguish than I could ever hope to make up for. However, once I started digesting all the literature I was typing and reading, I started taking a sincere interest in the Project Change program. I also started feeling the guilt associated with the wreckage of my past.

I found myself seriously considering a life without drugs and alcohol, rather than just a temporary abstinence until I got off parole. I started to really want it, not for me, but for my family. After Lynda started reading *my* letters, now rife with 12-Step clichés and jargon, her return letters were so full of hope, encouragement, and happiness, that I became much more determined to stay clean. She and my mom were so proud of me that I absolutely could not let them down after everything I had put them through.

A mother's love knows no bounds in many cases. When my mom

died, my aunt said, "Johnny, your mother idolized you. To her, the sun rose and set with you. There was nothing or nobody more important to her than you." My mom continued to enable me after her death. The inheritance she left provided me with enough money to finance two graduate degrees and enough for me to live comfortably since then. She went to her grave providing for the little boy she idolized. Today, I idolize her for giving me such unconditional love. She never lost faith in me. She loved me as much when I was drinking and using as she did when I was a kid, or after I got clean and sober.

In Project Change, we were taught that we had a disease that was chronic, progressive, and fatal; it was chronic because it never went away, progressive because it kept getting worse, and fatal because it killed people on a regular basis. We also learned about family dynamics such as codependency and we learned about the addictive personality, barriers to intimacy, anger management, and a special focus on relapse prevention. We did role playing in preparation for saying no. We covered a lot of the material that I used later as a Recovery Advocate in a drug rehabilitation center. Project Change worked for me. Within four months, I believed I had recovered from a seemingly hopeless case of mind and body. I was certain that I would not drink or use anymore. However, the fact is that even among those who are certain they will not drink or use anymore, most of them will anyway. So it was with me.

Kathy, one of the teachers in the program, recognized that I had academic ability and suggested I go to school when I got out. I said something like, "Yeah, yeah, sounds like a good idea." But I wasn't serious and she could see that. She approached me on the matter several times, practically nagging. Finally, I started giving it some serious consideration. I knew that I was going to be living with my mom again when I was released. She was on her last legs and I wanted to take care of her for what remained of her life. I figured going to school would keep me busy with homework when I was at home. Plus, I could be of help to my mom and, at the same time, be doing something for myself. When Kathy heard me talking this way, she started believing that I might be serious.

In Project Change, I learned that if lasting change is going to take place, one has to monitor and discipline their thought processes; therefore, if I was going to remain abstinent when I was released, I was going to have to change my thinking. As it was, almost every waking moment was spent thinking about either the bar where I was a bartender, how much fun scavenging at the dump was, the people I drank and used with, and all the women I slept with. I came to realize that being in a recovery-oriented environment and having this *stinking thinking* going on in my head at the same time was like having someone pushing me away and saying "come here" at the same time. I had to ask myself, *How can intrinsic recovery take place with such a conflict?*

All the great leaders throughout history have taught the principle that our life is the result of our thoughts. Buddha said, "A man's life is the direct result of his thoughts." Solomon said, "As a man thinks in his heart, so is he." Happiness comes from happy thoughts. That's another reason why I was relatively happy when I was drinking and using (or maybe I choose to only remember the good times). Success comes from successful thoughts, failure from failing thoughts. So, our life is controlled by our thinking.

Our minds have two parts, a conscious part and an unconscious part. The 'depth' component of depth psychology is the unconscious part. The conscious part is what we think and reason with, but the unconscious part controls bodily functions such as breathing, blood circulation, digestion; it never sleeps and is working all the time. It's like a computer. It takes in data and processes it. It has a memory of everything that has ever happened to us, from the day we were born to the present moment. It is non-judgmental. It doesn't know what is good or what is bad. It doesn't care whether the thoughts come from us or from others. If we don't make the effort to program it positively, our unconscious will take directions from other people, or from our environment, or from our own self-talk whether positive or negative. I used to wonder why I didn't always get what I wanted or why I couldn't do certain things. Perhaps I was sending negative messages to my unconscious, or maybe it picked up negative inputs from those around me. My dad always said that I was too easily influenced by my friends. I was.

One of the tenets of the Project Change program was: If our lives are not what we want, we have the power to *change* them. And we change them by changing our thoughts, which are programmed into our unconscious. So, I invented a methodology to change my thinking: I simply decided that I would *shoo away* my old thoughts and replace them with different thoughts. I did this quite literally. With my hand in a swishing motion by my ear, I shooed the recurring thoughts away and started thinking new, more positive thoughts. Walking around the prison's big yard shooing thoughts away in that manner, I could tell by the looks I was getting that I was being viewed through jaundiced eyes. "A nut case" I'm sure they must have thought. I didn't care. I was on the road to a new life without drugs and alcohol.

At first, it took me a long time to remember to shoo away my negative recurring thoughts, I only did it two or three times a day. As time passed, however, I started doing it more often and then even more often, until I was doing it a lot, maybe twenty to even forty times a day! That's when I was getting so many of "the looks" from other inmates. After a while, I discovered that I wasn't doing it as often. It started going back the other way. As time went on, I did this thought process less and less because I wasn't thinking the old thoughts as often anymore. Amazing, I had replaced them with new thoughts. And then, guess what? After about three or four months, I had exorcized all those old thoughts by replacing them with thoughts of what I really wanted to be doing and where I really wanted to be when I got out.

I stared to visualize myself in 12-Step meetings and I visualized myself in college classrooms. I also visualized spending time at home, taking care of my mom which, of course, served as further impetus to remain straight and sober. How could I be a comfort to my mother at the end of her life, if I was still drinking and using? Eventually, staying clean and sober had become the most important thing in my life, more important than having fun, even more important than my daughter and mother. Without total abstinence from drugs and alcohol, what good would I be to them? They may have been my incentive for *getting* clean, but *staying* clean finally became *my* top priority.

A couple of months before my release date, Kathy volunteered to help me with the tedious financial aid paperwork, so I could get the federal Pell Grant when I was released. I received the financial aid paperwork and she helped me with it like she had promised. I was forty-five years old and was going to be a college student again. I tried college twice in the early '60s, both of which were failures; so I came to accept that I wasn't college material. And maybe I wasn't, then.

My daughter had gotten clean and sober while I was doing time in the county jail, about a year before I went to prison. She still has the letters I wrote to her during that time, plus the ones I wrote from prison. After reading them again, I am amazed at all the fatherly advice I was giving her. Some of it was actually sound, but most of it was from a refractory and hedonistic loser with an inflated male ego. One thing was consistent in those letters, however: I never failed to tell her how proud I was of her and how much I loved her. If nothing else, she grew up knowing she was loved. And that, I believe, is the reason she is the epitome of motherhood to my two grandchildren today.

The letters she wrote to me were recovery-oriented and she mentioned several of my dope-fiend friends who were showing up in AA meetings. It was comforting to know that I was going to have friends at meetings when I got out. But since I considered myself more of a drug addict than an alcoholic (I never thought of alcohol as a drug), I planned on attending NA meetings. I eventually resolved to attend both.

Today, I own the home I grew up in and I have earned a few degrees culminating with a Doctorate Degree. But having a doctorate, owning my home, and having my car, truck, and camper paid for are not the things that make me happy. The closeness I share with my daughter and grandchildren makes me happy. Thinking about the time I spent caring for my mom before she died makes me happy. But, could I have sustained the happiness I had during childhood, adolescence, and through most of my drug and alcohol use, had I not stopped using? No. Why?

In my opinion, happiness is part of a temperament that is innate. Of course, life's circumstances can alter that, but I believe that the basic temperament is static. If trauma doesn't strike and we have had a stable and loving foundation in early childhood, most of us are capable of handling most of life's encumbrances. That's still my opinion, anyway. It is highly unlikely that I could have handled the mental, physical, and emotional encumbrances resulting from continued drug and alcohol use. I learned early in recovery that becoming responsible and accountable for our actions is a cornerstone of a life well lived.

— John S.

John S. is the father of Lynda S. in Chapter One. His book can be found in the Bibliography

"Serene I fold my hands and wait,
nor care for wind, nor tide, nor sea;
I rave no more 'against time or fate,
for lo, my own shall come to me."
—John Burroughs

While we strive to create our realities, sometimes we get side-tracked and find ourselves entering a darkened awareness filled with regret, pain, and depression. This is what seemed to happen to my son Richard each time he reached for that dream which kept reemerging within him to be a sober man. He strived to manifest a positive, productive life, but alcoholism always had its last word.

Within the realm of metaphysics, it is accepted that we each are co-creators of our reality along with that *Something More*. This universal law applies to all individuals, no matter what their religion or spiritual belief. By assuming responsibility for our life choices, we cannot *deny* responsibility for their outcomes. "What we sow, so shall we reap" is known throughout the world.

This premise of creating our own reality is in fact a Universal Truth and has been written, lectured, and handed-down through the centuries. One of the most recent and wide-spread written works is *The Secret* which has been displayed on the news, Oprah, and many other television programs. Another book first published in 1935 by George W. Plummer titled *Consciously Creating Circumstances* states much of the same language. Plummer belonged to a highly spiritual group called the "Society of Rosicrucians" which believes in many of the metaphysical laws which are widely known today. Plummer wrote about *thought-forms* and how we can use our mind's power together with spiritual intention to achieve our goals and to assist in humanity's evolution at the same time. He wrote:

> To become or to make one's self a chosen vessel implies a direct personal responsibility, one that we have not generally observed to be stressed by most self-help philosophies of the day, which are devoted mainly to the general subject of "How to get what you want." The correlative responsibility is To Use What You Get.
>
> There is a law back of all this. Forces in nature are in a state of constant flux—ebb and flow. The stream goes on continuously, with waves of action and reaction. If we keep on with our course, we ride the waves. If we drift, we move

around in circles with the counter waves, and get nowhere.

We cannot merely sit back and assume our meditating, praying, even begging God/Goddess/All That Is to bring us our desired outcomes will, in fact, reward our efforts. There is a reason for our human struggles, some of which is to realize our strength and inner power to overcome adversities; and some are present for our individual and human evolution. Ultimately, *struggle and suffering are products of our free will.*

Conquering our addictions may sound like a different story, it is not. When we allow our doubts and fears, pain, and woundedness to halt our attempts to overcome our addictions and suffering, we miss the life that could have been. It was Shakespeare who said, "Our doubts are traitors, and make us lose the good we oft might win, by fearing to attempt."

How does one begin to co-create their reality to rid themselves of addictions and life struggle? Einstein said often that we need to enjoy the faculty of our imaginations. He felt our imaginations, our dreams, thoughts, and visions were more important than knowledge. The use of thought and emotion through the Unknowable creates reality in unison with Divine guidance and our own free will; all these are crucial ingredients for manifesting a positive and addiction-free life. If we use our spiritual resources available to us, such as meditation, dreams, prayers, mindfulness, intuition, chanting, and ritual to enlist the guidance of that Something More, our lives can be directed to destinations we cannot imagine.

Another old but always accurate book, *Three Magic Words* by U.S. Anderson, first published in 1954, tells us the same magic in co-creating our reality is instilled within our souls. Anderson explains:

> *You've got to think success to be successful.* No one was ever successful by thinking failure. No one was ever a failure by thinking success. It is that simple. And the tool which we must use to prevent negative circumstance from entering our lives is that of faith.

There have been and are many spiritual masters walking this earth. If we listen to their words and their guidance, a new world will unfold. I have always encouraged my children to use the power of their minds to help guide them toward their dreams. I know my son did this often, seeking his sobriety many times through positive thinking and his faith in that Something More. Keeping faith we will succeed. Keeping our thoughts, actions, and reactions in a positive mode and following the Divine Golden Rule, "Do unto others as we would have them do unto us," we allow the greater Universal Power to act for our benefit.

Rich's Story (continued)

When I was twenty-four years old, my Dad moved back to southern California for the work and Mom stayed up north for a while. My life got back on track, but I was still drinking regularly. I went to work for a couple of flooring shops, working with my Dad half the time. My life seemed to have been revived from the loneliness I had suffered while living alone. I was doing so well that I bought a ski boat; everyone was amazed at how well I was doing. But as I remember, my drinking got worse. The amount of whisky I was drinking was more than it ever had been. I was a "functioning alcoholic" and could wake-up at four o'clock in the morning and go to work. I was also working a lot of nights with my Dad. We worked in super-markets laying tile floors and making really good money.

This is when I started drinking regularly at work; I mean the hard stuff right off the shelves in the liquor department of the grocery stores. Yes, I was getting drunk as I was laying tile at night, and in the day. At this time, I think my Dad knew of my drinking only some of the time. My bosses didn't even have a clue yet; only the people that I directly worked with knew of my drinking.

At this time in my life, my Mom and Dad had gotten remarried after being divorced for about eight years. Mom moved back down south to be with my Dad and this is the time she started to find out about my problem with alcohol. Being a counselor, she always tried to "doctor-me," and she "mothered-me" at the same time. But I didn't want to listen to her. She made me mad, so I just kept on drinking, still denying to her that I was an alcoholic. My drinking alone every day had gotten worse and I found myself isolating myself from my parents and my friends. I spent most of my time out in the garage, working on my truck and building engines. This became a hobby for me, plus, I could drink all I wanted whenever I wanted.

Me and my Mom were not getting along very well at all now; we constantly fought. I look back at this time and know that I was a full-blown alcoholic then. I think maybe I was drinking so hard to cover up my real feelings that I had for my Mom which was anger for leaving me when my parents got divorced. Also, I didn't know how to live as a whole family again. It seems to me that my life just went up and down constantly and never balanced out. My Mom did all that she could to help me, like getting my driver's license back which wasn't easy. But I would only let her help me with the things I wanted help with, so I feel I may have used her to get certain things for myself.

Then after about a year, we started to get along with one another and I was doing a lot of things for my parents. I knew they wanted to sell the house. Together with my Dad, I painted the house inside and out; put in new floors; a new roof; and, completed the landscape. But, my drinking was getting even worse. I was back and forth with my jobs and during this whole time, my Dad never had much to say about my problem with alcohol. My Mom did, but I didn't want to listen to her. I thought there was nothing wrong and I didn't want to talk about it. I would just walk away from her or get angry when she tried to talk to me.

In those years, my Mom's family would have everyone over for Christmas and Thanksgiving Holidays. I wouldn't show up at all. I guess I was afraid of what everyone would think of me and I didn't want the family to tell me that I had a problem with alcohol. Another reason was that they might not let me drink when I came over and just the thought of that possibility made me mad; so I did not go. Now, I know that they care for me very much and they missed seeing me on all those holidays.

When I was about twenty-five years old, I remember losing my "Class A" driver's license that I had worked so hard to get. I was coming home from the bar at about eleven o'clock at night and got pulled over. I passed all the tests but I blew a .08 into the breathalyzer, so they booked me but released me within twenty minutes. I lost my driver's license for one year and paid a fine of one hundred dollars. This hurt me a lot. Also, I had to sell my ski boat to pay for my attorney's fees, and that sucked. This was the beginning of my losing everything again.

I could not drive to work anymore, so I had to turn a lot of work down. I was still working with my Dad when I could at this time. I was still a very functional alcoholic. I still didn't think I had a problem with my drinking. Even though I didn't *physically* need to drink every day, I thought that drinking would make me feel better. I believe this is when I was drinking about a fifth of vodka every day; I changed my drink to vodka. I don't remember why I changed my drink; maybe because I found out that vodka was cheaper to buy than whisky!

Around age twenty-six, I felt I was getting my drinking under control. I started working full-time again for a flooring shop, laying tile floors in grocery stores and other commercial buildings, making plenty of money again. I felt good. I got my first cellular phone and pager, and bought a new truck. I had to fire a friend that I had as an apprentice working for the shop. He was too hung-over in the mornings to go to work, or he was always late. Also, he didn't want to work nights, all because of his alcohol problem. So, my boss hired another friend of mine. We worked together for a couple of years; then both of us started to drink regular again, stopping at bars at all hours of the day, and also drinking on the job. But we were always there and never late. Then we both got to where we physically could not make it to work. First he was laid-off; then in a few months, I also was laid-off. But before this all happened, my Mom and Dad sold the family house and I had to move into an apartment.

I stayed in my apartment for six months and worked laying floors to pay my rent and my bills, but mostly I drank very hard and alone. I was hurt that my parents sold the house; that I had to move out; that I lost my previous job; and, that I had to sell one of my trucks. At this time, I started to isolate myself for days at a time and get drunk, and then sleep it off. I didn't want to do anything at all. I now realize that I was feeling sorry for myself.

At this time, I still didn't want to admit I was an alcoholic and that all of my problems were because of my drinking every day and not following through with my responsibilities. Things got worse and these six months were some of my worst times ever. I had no food, no gasoline, and no money, but I still made sure I had just enough money to get drunk and to pay my bar tab. Many times, my friends took care of me. They fed me, gave me a few dollars here and there, bought my gasoline, and most of them were no better off than I was. It was like many of us kids who grew up together just fell into a hole at the same time, and it was all because of alcohol.

6 *The Spiritual Path*

> "We don't need more money, we don't need greater success or fame, we don't need the perfect body or even the perfect mate—right now, at this very moment, we have a mind, which is all the basic equipment we need to achieve complete happiness."
>
> —His Holiness The Dalai Lama

I have read hundreds of books. It is amazing to me how authors use the exact same words to form their pose. Sometimes, these words lay dormant on the page while others instigate mind-visions. It reminds me of the difference between an addiction story written while visiting a recovery center fresh off the drug of choice and one written several months or years post-sobriety. You may notice the difference in writing between many of the addiction stories in this book. Some stories, like my son's, were written while in recovery programs, while others were written well into the recovery process.

When I read the addiction story of Augusten Burroughs in his memoir *Dry*, I found myself wanting to write with more humor and a sense of uncaring abandon. Burroughs brings to his reader all the pertinacity of a bulldog laced with a tinge of self-deprecation. One particularly notable tale I savor reads:

> I call 411 for …Proud Institute. I scribble the number on my hand; then go to the refrigerator for another ale.
>
> After I hang up, I walk into the bathroom and look in the mirror. "What have you done? Man, are you fucking crazy?" I watch myself take a sip of ale. "You don't even like ale," I tell my reflection. My reflection takes another gulp and goes back to the refrigerator.

I'm expected at Proud Institute in three days. I have a reservation, as if I am simply going to Shutters on the Beach in Santa Monica.

I go into the living room and sit on the sofa; I stare at the blank wall across from me. Suddenly, rehab doesn't seem so fun after all...

The lawn has been worn away to bare dirt from heavy foot traffic. And the sign in front is missing a few letters. It reads:

P O U   INS   T   E

Signs with missing letters can only mean bad things. When I was a kid, the "e" went out in the local Price Chopper grocery store and stayed out for many years. Because the "Pric Chopper" logo happened to be a man wielding an axe; the sign sent out an eerie and powerful castration message, which, at the age of twelve, affected me deeply.

Burroughs' wry humor sticks to my ribs. Did Burroughs find his spiritual path, that Something More, on his recovery journey? I cannot say. He didn't mention a Higher Power or a God to pray to or some other Force to assume his sobriety. Perhaps Burroughs found a sense of freedom, a release in his writing; release from the past, the guilt, or the victimhood that comes wrapped with blinders hanging limp at the nose like a pair of old reading glasses. I recommend reading *Dry*, only if to find a piece of yourself in his words, which stream from lines of prose and humor and pain.

∽∽

Rich's Story (continued)

When I was twenty-seven, I moved out of my apartment and into a tiny house in my hometown. I started back to work, laying floors for my old boss by myself. My neighbor and very good friend, Jim, was also my landlord. We lived on twenty acres of land that he owned. Jim was an alcoholic also and we got along very well. I used to go to him and talk about all kinds of things; he knew that I was an alcoholic.

While I lived there, the first six months were very good to me. I was working doing floors and also helping Jim out on the property. My drinking had slowed down, though I was drinking a pint of bourbon every other day. Also, Jim and I drank beer together every day. I did not find myself getting drunk or sick, just enjoying life. Jim taught me wood-working in his shop. I was having a lot of fun learning how to do this, along with all the other things I got to do living on a ranch.

I do believe I was feeling free from all my problems that had occurred when I was living alone in the apartment. This country lifestyle was me and I liked it. My drinking problem seemed not to exist, even though I was still drinking. Maybe it was because I wasn't alone anymore. Jim was like a dad to me and we had a strong friendship. After living there for six months, my boss had to lay me off and I started to work right in town, plowing fields and cutting down trees for firewood.

With staying at home to work, there was more time on my hands. This is when I remember my drinking becoming more steady once again. I was drinking a pint every day and functioning with no physical problems, always up early and working hard. Then the hangovers started all over again, and I was drinking to get well, to feel better. Jim noticed this right away and had to start waking me up in the mornings so that I would get up and get the day started. He would always tell me that I needed to get outside and start moving around to get rid of the hangovers; he was right.

Now that I could handle the pain of drinking every day and was able to work, I started to drink even more, a fifth a day was normal for me once again. My alcoholic friends were coming over all the time now and I was employing some of them, as well as Jim. There was a lot of hard liquor and beer around me. I even slowed down going to the bar because of this. My friends drank just like me, so I would buy two bottles and we drank all day long during work.

Slowly, I realized that my money was disappearing; my bills were not getting paid; and I found the gas gauge in my truck on empty quite often. But, I still had a full bottle of whisky or vodka every day. Not having gasoline didn't bother me because I worked at home and I didn't have to drive a lot. I feel all of these factors caused me to isolate myself from the world and only communicate with my friends and firewood customers. I was drinking by myself more than I ever had done before.

Jim started getting mad at me for my heavy drinking. I was not paying my monthly rent, so he suggested that I take care of his property and that would be my rent payment. I figured this was great; now I had more money in my pocket to spend on liquor! Eventually, Jim asked me to leave because of my alcoholism. We remained good friends and saw each other often. He managed to stay sober for another year, and then he relapsed. Soon he died an alcohol related death.

After leaving Jim's, I had a car wreck and got a DUI for the second time. I voluntarily went to St. John of God's Recovery program to *get it* with my alcoholism. I admitted I was an alcoholic. Being there, I learned a lot and did my 12-Steps of AA for the first time. These tools helped me get back into society and when I left, I landed a good job in a machine shop. I was living with my parents most of this time again. I did stay sober for six months but stopped going to meetings and didn't talk to my sponsor. I thought that I could do it on my own. I was wrong.

Some of my notes from yet another Rehab:

...Beginning a new detox and rehab program today, I had a potent dream last night about a unicorn. Mom gave me a writing Journal with a unicorn on the cover to write down my feelings while I am here. I will write in it all the time now. I am at the time in my life where I want to change. The unicorn is a great sign to me for transformation; I have already started my journey.

...So far, I have been sober for thirty-seven days in this center. Being here is an experience of spiritual change, like a constant ongoing Life inside of me. I have yet to let my inner-Self run outside of my-self, wild and free completely.

...Today, I read my first Step: I am "powerless over alcohol and my life is unmanageable." My reading is very good now, especially standing up in front of a lot of people. Maybe that's because my anxiety is not controlling me anymore. I have been free of panic attacks completely. I feel super!

...Today, I had a twenty-four hour pass to go to court for my DUI. My fine is one thousand dollars and three years probation.

...Today, I got a buddy in the program. His name is Dan; he's an alcoholic-addict. He is learning his way around. He has lifted my spirits in an enlightening way.

...Well, this week I got sick. It's been hard to focus on the program and follow the Steps. Sunday I will get to see Mom and Dad for a seven-hour pass.

...Today, I am sixty days sober; this time I really do feel the change within my inner-Self, unlike the last time when I was over four months sober. Then there was no change in my personality and thinking. Now, I open up more to my Self and others. I write, read, and talk around with new people all the time.

...I saw something that I have been checking each day, a female dove sitting on her eggs in a nest. She has been here for two weeks now. I think I am the only one who has seen this; I hope to get to see her babies this spring.

...I can't believe how many cigarettes all the people smoke here, around four to five hundred a day; that's a lot. I guess the alcohol or drugs were a lot worse. I have stopped smoking for a month at a time, but I always stated again when I stopped drinking. I think my behavior and addictive personality is changing more every day, I am down to four or five cigs a day right now. I know that one day my life can and will be manageable by giving my addictions to God.

...Got a new sponsor today, Steve. He seems pretty cool.

...Just got back from Goal Class. Writing down my goals took about three hours! I care a lot about my sobriety and my program; they are both the most important things in my life right now.

...Understanding my Steps in the AA program this time around sure makes it different being and living sober. I now see that it is possible for me to stay clean and enjoy it! Not like the first time I got sober when all I did was stop drinking alcohol and that just made me a miserable son-of-a-bitch. I was just a dry-drunk. That lifestyle is just as bad as when I was still drinking every day!

...Today, I realized that the dream of the unicorn was an experience of my spirituality deep within myself. The transformation from old to new is happening every day inside and outside myself. I remember some very special moments that I would have when I was very young. At that time, I knew God was with me. I understood what these experiences were but never told anyone about them. I now know that they were spiritual experiences.

...This week, all the residents and counselors went to the park and had a picnic. We played volley ball and football. While we were there, one guy found a bag of heroin by the tables. Everyone was freaking-out about it and what to do with it. We gave it to one of the counselors and he threw it in the trash can. I feel proud of us all for not "doing-it" and getting high. My volley ball team won two games; that was a fun day.

...Yesterday, I had a meeting with my sponsor and he is going to help me get a place to live at the sober living house for when I leave here. I worked my fourth Step, a hard one. Steve is a hard-ass of a sponsor. I am strong today in my sobriety.

...Today is ninety days of sobriety for me. Next week I will get my chip. Now I am not so sure I want Steve to be my sponsor. I know I need help but Steve isn't around enough to answer my questions.

...Right now, I have a feeling of wholeness. This must be because I did a thorough goal sheet this week. Just writing in my Journal is a small accomplishment for me, but it feels good.

...I love carrying around my Journal to write in. We just got back from an AA club meeting; what a super meeting it was! I feel great. I read chapter five in the Big Book and shared for a good while in front of everyone. I call myself Dick to be anonymous. By sharing our Steps with each other, we may relieve a little of that blockage from our past and learn that it is okay to be an alcoholic or addict because of what we went through. Forgiveness is the answer.

...I worked in the detox room today. Hard to see the new guys like this.

...Lots of people leaving now, their time here is over. Good to see most of them with smiles on their faces. I said a prayer for each one as they left and hope to see them again.

...Tonight I received my ninety day chip. I feel good that I have accomplished this. This chip represents a lot of hard work. My life is changing a lot and it is all for the best. I am feeling calm and relaxed right now; it's a beautiful night.

...My sobriety is growing stronger all the time. Working the 12-Steps is becoming easier every day. I can't believe how simple they really are; the more I read, the more that is revealed to me. I can feel God inside of me more each day. I am now a senior resident. New guys are coming to me for help and direction; it is an honor for me to be able to help someone. I am excited to be a sponsor one day.

...This week went by fast. I feel I am well focused on my program and learning well. It is simple, but not easy. I know I will be one of the few that stay sober and keep recovering one day at a time.

...Today, I visited the sober living house where I will be staying for a while. There is one room available now, I hope to get it. I never thought I would be doing something like this in my life—what a trip!

...One more week to go! My sobriety is one hundred and seven days strong. This place has taught me a lot about myself and my disease, which is alcoholism. With the knowledge I have received here, there is a very good chance that I will stay sober for a long time, I hope.

...Today, I moved into the sober living house. I hope to find a job around here; the rent is $45 each week. Tomorrow, I will walk or take the bus around to find a job.

"Part of the understanding of these people is to realize that often what's under the veneer of who or what they're presenting (an image or a persona) is quite possibly another Edgar Alan Poe, Carl Jung, or Vincent van Gogh. But first they need to clean up and put an end to being thought of, and thinking of themselves as, scumbag sewer rats."

—John E. Smethers

Alcoholism is a wretched disease. It attacks all aspects of the soul; emotional, physical, psychological, and spiritual. Many times, if there is a firm spiritual belief (not necessarily religious) in place, the addict or alcoholic can move into sobriety, knowing he is forgiven for missing his life's proverbial mark. Rich was baptized in the Christian faith. He proudly allowed the minister to dunk his entire upper body in a bath of blessed water for all to witness. As parents, we were glad our son had chosen his spiritual path and congratulated him with praise and hugs. He was living in a residential rehabilitation facility at the time, working diligently to rid his mind, body, and soul of his alcoholic demon.

Much has been said about addicts looking to a Higher Power to find a type of salvation which only another addict understands is pertinent. I am sure there is a bond between addicts even if unknown to one another; I see it in their eyes. One time, Rich shared with me his *Big Book* (Alcoholics Anonymous) given to him many years ago by another alcoholic. After the Introduction written by William Silkworth, M.D., Rich wrote these words:

The doctor's word is very right.
We are a very different people.
Those that will give their time to help us
May God Bless All of Them
Amen, Amen
We do have a desire of some kind.
I hope that one day we will all be helped
And cared for respectfully,
After all we are human.
Richard Sinor
And All Alcoholics

Richard's struggle with alcoholism is typical, not special. My struggle with Rich's alcoholism *is* special; he is my son.

In his latest book *Against the Stream*, Noah Levine tells us his answer to the question, "What was the first experience that made *you* think that the spiritual path was possible?" He writes that he had been drinking and getting high since he was twelve years old and facing yet another felony arrest. It was in a moment of clarity that brought a spiritual experience in which he could no longer blame others for his life choices, choices which caused him and others much pain and suffering, that urged him to become a Buddhist. Practicing meditation, prayer, and looking deeply into his addictive behavior, Noah learned for the first time that he had hope.

I have hope for my son; I pray he feels hope too.

When I published my "Call for Addiction Stories," I did not ask for *spiritually orientated* stories. However, as you can surmise, most of the stories submitted include some type of metaphysical, religious, or spiritual component. Reaching for that Something More to guide one on their recovery journey just feels right somehow. For Richard, his strong belief in a Higher Power is a necessary facet to his unfolding journey. Below are the words on a card Rich carries in his Big Book to help him remember he is not alone:

> What if you had all the help you needed to wake up
> From your dreams of fear and find your way back home
> To the heart of love? What if you could ask for and
> Receive help from both the seen and the unseen worlds?

All the help I need
Is available for me.
I can receive it by asking.

—Joan Borysenko

What lies behind us and what lies before us are tiny matters compared to what lies within us.
—Oliver Wendell Holmes

The Gift of Life

As I write this, I am a fifty-four-year-old woman. I started drinking and using drugs at the tender age of fourteen. At first, it all started by my older brothers making me drink a can of beer so I wouldn't tell my parents on them; I would have gotten into trouble too. Then it continued with peer pressure, you know the kind, "Hey, everyone is doing it." But as the years went on, and at the age of forty-nine, I found myself with a gun to my head. I did not think I could go one day without drinking. I was sick of myself and sick of living.

Drinking and using drugs was the only way of life for me. It was a full-time job. I hated it but my body craved it, every single day. I could see no other way out.

As I was contemplating doing something that went against everything I was taught as a child, I said, "God Please Help Me." The next thing I knew, I was on the phone with my twin sister who then made a call to our older sister who just happened to be in Florida. She explained to our older sis what was going on. My older sister called me and asked me if I was ready to quit. She would give me the "Gift of Life" so to speak. I told her I was more than ready. She called around to a few rehab centers and the next day, she and my mom traveled three hours to pick me up and we went to the Lisa Merlin House in Orlando.

I stayed there in long-term residential treatment for thirteen months and for nine months of aftercare treatment. I just celebrated my sixth year of being clean and sober. It's truly a *miracle*. God has His plan for us and mine was to remain on this earth a little while longer.

— Judy S.

> *Doubt is a pain too lonely to know*
> *that faith is his twin brother.*
>
> —Kahlil Gibran

Can you envision the thread which weaves between the lines of the stories so far? It sparkles in many; in some, it covertly shines but is present all the same. The thread is that spiritual spark of Something More. There rests within these stories an awakening of the spiritual; it is noted even in those who have not yet chosen to surrender their addictive habit but have decided to share their journey nonetheless. Even the stories from friends and family members, whose loved ones silently pull the darkness of addiction over their lives, declare an element of spiritual grace.

Many substance abuse treatment programs try to incorporate a sense of spirituality, some as a major focal point, although staunchly religious. When individuals make that initial decision to obtain help to quit using drugs or alcohol, have they also reached their spiritual peak? If so, can we encourage this direction?

One way to touch your Higher Power, God/Goddess/All That Is, Higher-Self is to quiet the clutter in your mind and listen meditatively for just a few minutes. Listen for that voice inside which can bring both peace and chaos. What is important in doing this exercise is not hearing what the voice is saying but that you *realize you are not the voice*. Eckhart Tolle, Oprah's famous guru of 2008, whose writing has brought millions to a place of stillness to listen within, writes in *Stillness Speaks*:

> "When you notice that voice, you realize that who you are is not the voice—the thinker—but the one who is aware of it."

The soul is that part of you that is witnessing *you* listening to that small still voice. To know your soul is to find direction. This is the message in which the addiction stories speak so clearly.

In my book *An Inspirational Guide for the Recovering Soul*, you can begin to search your inner-Self to find the soul longing to be noticed. First, hold the book closed and allow yourself to roam your mind for just the right issue to explore. Then open it to any page to find jewels of insight and inspiration which can lead to your soul's journey. One such passage reads:

> Avoiding pain can lead to more pain. Perhaps it is time to really examine your issues. Pain either comes from outside

yourself such as a trauma which you can/cannot control or from the inside, as a self-induced suffering. One way to examine pain—whether it is anger, pity, guilt, fear, or confusion—is to ask yourself this question: *How would I counsel or advise another person in the same situation?*

This examination begins with the understanding that there is always another person with very similar circumstances. Imagine yourself in the counselor's chair this time. You are listening patiently to this person's problems and worries, acknowledging their emotions with a sense of empathy. As you begin to unravel the circumstances they have presented to you, allow your mind to wander and search for direction and answers which you can relate back to them. You may wish to make a list of these ideas your inner guidance is giving you to help this person.

Allow yourself to be the witness and the guidance will follow.

7 Searching for Recovery

"The starting point is the Self. Its essence is water. Only clarity, willingness to change, is effective now. A correct relationship to your self is primary, for from it flow all possible correct relationships with others and with the Divine."

The Book of Runes

Doing our best can be a profound effort when it comes to most situations in our lives. If we do our best, we feel a sense of success, a sense of triumph that comes from knowing we "gave it our all." In the area of addictions, only those addicted can personally weigh whether their best effort was achieved toward a recovery goal. Just quitting drug use or ceasing to drink alcohol is only the beginning of recovery. As we discussed earlier, long-term recovery entails a gambit of actions, behaviors, and tolerances including a sense of self-acceptance, self-forgiveness, and forgiveness of others. It is evident that many addicts work at giving up drugs their entire life. Can "working on" be the same as *in* recovery? If one is *in recovery* but still using or drinking once-in-a-while, are they doing their best to obtain sobriety?

Striving to do our best not only takes effort, it requires patience—patience and time to understand why we have chosen the decisions which led to the outcomes we are experiencing. Some people do not have the luxury of time; some have no patience to uncover and discover the true reasons for their behavior. They continue their self-testing, telling themselves they will quit after the stress eases up or the holidays are over. These individuals are the ones who could benefit from our helping hand and understanding ear. "If by the grace of God, there go I" is a lesson well learned.

Anyone can develop a habit, a pattern, or an addiction. A passionate advocate for addicts of all kinds is the director of the National Institute of Drug Abuse (NIDA) Dr. Nora Volkow. Volkow says brain science is proving that we all have the potential to become addicted to something: drugs, alcohol, tobacco, sex, gambling, even food. Also, researchers are learning that all addictions are more alike than was previously thought. Becoming an addict is more a matter of chance than we ever realized; mix the right combination of genetics and life experience, and anyone could find him or herself addicted to something. (*Newsweek*, Dec/Jan 2006)

Knowing that we all have the propensity to develop an addictive behavior or habit is a bit scary; however, answer a few questions below and you might change your mind if you think you are not at risk for developing an addiction.

- Do you park your car in the same space at work?

- Do you brush your teeth the same way each time?

- Are there set programs on your DVR to watch each week?

- When you go to a certain fast-food restaurant, do you order the same meal?

- How many times have you fixed a dinner exactly the same way?

- How many times have you driven the same route to work?

Well, I don't need to ask more questions; you get the idea.

Our brains work the same way; they become addicted to certain patterns, reactions, and influences. Actually, using cocaine and falling in love stimulate the same brain centers; emotional love and using cocaine produce very similar neuro-activity in the brain. No wonder it's difficult to give up drugs!

Normally, the brain produces levels of a chemical called dopamine which balance our emotions somewhere between excitement and depressive moods. When your brain is on drugs, the dopamine transporters and receptors act in abnormal ways. Here are a few examples:

- Cocaine: blocks the brain's transporters causing over-stimulation of the cells.

- Alcohol: causes brain cells to react with inhibitory neuro-transmitters and prevents cells from becoming excited or registered at all. Alcohol affects areas of the brain involving memory, impulse control, and decision-making.

- Marijuana: mimics the brain's function of releasing inhibitors but it is also involved in removing unnecessary short-term memories and slowing down physical movement.

- Methamphetamines: mimic dopamine in the brain cells and this excess causes over-stimulation. Meth is highly addictive, making the user feel intense pleasure.

- Heroin: mimics our natural opiates in the brain, turning-off dopamine inhibition. There is a flood of dopamine to the cell synapses producing feelings of sedation and the dulling of pain.

(Learn Genetics™ "The Mouse Party" from the University of Utah)

❧

I met Dr. Wayne Dyer long ago at a workshop I was attending. His presence is that of a master of human understanding. His words stream from his mouth uninterrupted like water flowing from a fountain. Dyer's book *The Power of Intention: Learning to Co-create Your World Your Way* is filled with quotes and lengthy lectures; yet, somehow I found myself turning the final pages, looking for more. Within the entire book, I found no other insight as valuable to me as when he discovered that, "...intention is not something *you do*, but rather a force that exists in the universe as an invisible field of energy." Yes, we can have good intentions and develop our ability to use our thoughts for such intentions, but real intention is an unseen force which allows our thoughts to manifest. It is not our will but that Something More which allows our intentions to manifest through our freewill.

I am reminded of a parable I read in *The Four Agreements* by Don Miguel Ruiz about a man who wanted to transcend his suffering.

> He went to a Buddhist temple to find his answers. He asked a master, "If I mediate for four hours each day, how long would it take for me to be free of my suffering?"
>
> The master replied, "If you meditate four hours, you will transcend your suffering in ten years."
>
> Well, the man thought he could do more and asked the master, "If I mediate each day for eight hours, how long will it take?"

The master said, "If you meditate eight hours a day, you will transcend in twenty years."

"What?" asked the man, "why will it take me longer if I meditate more?"

The master replied, "You are not here in this life to sacrifice your joy and life. You are here to live and be happy and to love! If you can do your best in two hours of meditation but you spend eight hours instead, you will become too tired to live your life. Do your best and then you will learn that it does not matter how long you meditate; what matters is that you live, and love, and be happy."

So, we continue to do our best today and tomorrow, and live our lives in love and happiness.

An Addict Pharmacist's Journey to Recovery

I was born in eastern Kentucky to my wonderful, loving, and Christian parents. Neither of them drank or used drugs. Along with my older sister and brother, we were your typical middle class family, free of the dysfunctions common to many alcoholic/ addict memoirs. In high school, I became fond of drinking alcohol and by college I could shotgun a beer faster than any human being on the planet. As a young man, I loved drinking and pursued it with passion.

In 1996, I graduated from the University of Kentucky, College of Pharmacy. Upon receiving the keys to the candy store, I quickly discovered the ease and comfort produced by ingesting the narcotics readily at my disposal. I remember well the day I took my first narcotic pill while at work. I had been practicing at my new job for only a few weeks and decided that perhaps a pill might help take the edge off. Moments later, I was a new man. I was happier, friendlier, more energetic, funnier, better looking, and downright invincible. A love affair had begun.

Within a short time, I was completely dependent on narcotics to get through a day. While still oblivious to the notion that I had a substance abuse problem, the complicated game of hiding my drug use from my family, my wife, and my employer began. My wife, Darcey, had never been fond of drinking and frequently admonished me for getting drunk. At this point, she was still clueless about my new narcotic hobby.

After less than a year-and-a-half of practicing pharmacy, I suffered my first serious consequence of addiction. In July of 1997, I was arrested by State Police and FBI agents for stealing drugs. They showed up on a Friday morning, read me my rights, and then led me out of the pharmacy in handcuffs while the local news crew filmed on. I was charged with three federal drug-related crimes which threatened to imprison me for ten-to-twenty years. My next memory is being processed at the Boyd County Detention Center in Ashland where they showed me to my accommodations in solitary confinement. I stayed there for five days until my detention hearing.

Released on bond, I spent the next three months awaiting my trial and drinking as much vodka as I could get my hands on. I drank every day to evade the anxiety and fear of the nightmare my life had turned in to. On day two of my trial, the prosecutor offered a plea bargain in which I would plead guilty to one count of obtaining a controlled substance by deception. I would receive four weekends in jail and three years federal probation.

One month later, I took a new job in a new town. Within weeks, I began drinking and using again. Still, I had no inkling that I was an addict. Gradually, I grew more and more dependent upon drugs to make it through the day and drank often at night. By the summer of 2000, my family and coworkers began to notice that something was wrong. My family organized an intervention where I admitted having a drug problem, but promptly refused to go to any treatment program. I would defeat addiction on my own. It's an option that all addicts want to try first, but it seldom works. By October, I was struggling terribly. Entire work days were lost to drug-induced blackouts. I tried several times to quit, but failed miserably over and over again.

One slow evening at the pharmacy, while my assistant was on break, I got down on my knees between the shelves of drugs. I prayed a desperate prayer, asking for God's help. A few days later, I was arrested again and led out of pharmacy job number two in handcuffs. In jail, on this divinely inspired incarceration, I felt a change took place. As I paced around the jail cell panic-stricken, defeated, and alone, I said aloud, "I'm an alcoholic and a drug addict and I don't have to keep living this way." Night turned to day, from desperation to celebration. I felt a weight lifted as hope entered.

From there, I went to a treatment facility outside Nashville called Cumberland Heights. After a short stay at home following rehab, I moved to a halfway house in Lexington, Kentucky where I would continue learning how to live without drugs and alcohol while avoiding jail time. I've not found it necessary to abuse drugs or alcohol since October 7, 2000, and I recently celebrated eight years of sobriety.

My license to practice pharmacy was suspended for six months following the arrest, but I was reinstated in July of 2001. I have successfully practiced pharmacy since then. Today my life is remarkably different. I live my life, instead of just surviving it day to day. I love my children more than my next breath and they never have to see their daddy drunk, high, or being arrested again. My wife is a jewel. She suffered through many stressful years of my active addiction and today is my best friend and a committed supporter of my recovery.

— Jared C.

Jared's book can be found in the Bibliography

"Affirm that you are inwardly guided by the Supreme Intelligence of the Universe. Affirm that everything you ought to know, you do know. Affirm that you are compelled to make right decisions. Know that there is something within you that will not permit you to make a mistake."

—Ernest Holmes

Resisting our present reality will not bring us any closer to our desired reality. In fact, resistance is the glue that keeps us stuck in the very circumstances we most want to change. *What you resist persists.* This means that when we resist something, the Universe actually sends more of it for us to deal with! An example might be you make a statement that you will definitely quit smoking cigarettes tomorrow. You prepare by throwing away the ones you have and set the ashtrays in the back drawer. You resist going to buy more for several hours; then your boss calls and tells you, you are fired! This is your test. Your stomach turns flips as you begin to seek your old friend. Marching out the door to buy more cigarettes, you resisted only to give in when your reality changed unexpectedly.

The same is true with any condition in our lives. Debbie Ford continues to enlighten us with her wise words, "Anything we want to change, anything we're afraid of, anything we refuse to accept causes internal resistance and sets us up for more pain and struggle. When we are in resistance, all our precious energy is being used to avoid what we do not want rather than to create what we do want."

The solution is simple: Surrender to your life exactly as it is. Surrender is a sacred practice that challenges us to dissolve our judgments and make peace with all that we have erroneously created. Ford declares, "If you feel any resistance to surrendering your resistance, just remember this: Resistance equals struggle, and surrender equals serenity. You have the power to choose between the two."

My Story (continued)

Much of the time while living in our old home, and then again when we moved into our new one, Rich tried hard to make a positive life for himself. He secured different jobs, mostly construction work, and I believe he found a bit of peace within himself. Maybe I was naïve; maybe I was just trying to make my own life work; but we seemed to connect in ways which brought us closer.

During this time, I continued my private practice and my writing. I was busy and preoccupied. I chose to wear blinders when it came to my son. When Rich crashed my car and almost killed himself, the blinders came off. The doctor told him if he did not stop drinking, he would die within a year. My heart sank and my insides lurched. This was the beginning of his several attempts at abstinence in rehabilitation programs, and subsequent relapses.

David and I joined Al-Anon and tried to stop enabling our son so he could hit his proverbial "bottom." We stretched our limits of tolerance many-times-over, desperately wanting Rich to "get it" and finally get off his addiction merry-go-round. Several times, we had to call the police to have him hauled from our doorstep due to his drunken condition; or, we rushed him to the hospital for medical care. With our own lives to sustain, we finally realized we could no longer *help* our son. Rich would need to find his own way, even if that meant seeing him only when he was sober.

Rich's Story (continued)

The end of one Rehab Journal:

...Today I got to be the secretary of an AA meeting; this is a privilege.

...I can't find work here. I am going to move back down the hill and work with a friend of mine near my folks. I will learn how to live sober for the first time in my life.

...Now I am back and it has been a super couple of months being here at Mom's and Dad's. We have a very close family relationship now. I was very disappointed that the job I wanted didn't work out but I am still happy and growing more every day.

...Well, I drank because of being laid-off work. I am detoxing; this sucks.

...I started AA meetings again. God, I need your help to get sober and stay sober again. I must be honest with myself and others to complete a new set of Steps. Today, I will make amends to the ones I have hurt yet again. When Mom gets home, I hope she will help me go over my Steps. God, I love you, thanks for the wisdom you have given me to know the difference.

...While going through those last withdrawals, it has been very hard for me to sleep. As long as I don't drink it will go away. Had a bad case of the "jitters" too, which always happens when I drink alcohol, then stop. Right now, it is hard for me to do anything; I am weak and tired.

...It's been a long time since I wrote in this Journal. Mom and Dad are helping me build my life again. Now that we are a family again, life has been hard, but rewarding. I drink on and off now. Work comes and goes; nothing permanent, which is depressing me.

...It's been one year since I entered the last rehab center. It has been a long ride that has been very hard. I see my writing changing; hard to write now. I am living with my cousin and her husband; bless them.

...Two years have gone by now since I have written. I drank a lot, played a lot, and cried a lot. Now it is time to move on. I don't care what the world thinks of me or that I am an alcoholic. Why did I even try to change; it was not for me. That is why my life went downhill and I got so lost. Now I will just be an alcoholic; that's who I am.

* * *

I have now been in my recovery from alcoholism for three years and have relapsed many times. The last four months in this recovery program, my third, have been the most successful that I have had. My first relapse, I had no idea why or how it happened. I know now what to look for and recognize before a possible relapse occurs. These will be the signs I will need to take action with and do not ignore. The key for me is not to lean on my own understanding, but to obey my Higher Power's will for me. No matter how much I do not want to obey, I must, because my sobriety comes first.

Recovery for me will be an ongoing commitment for the rest of my life. If I am going to stay sober, *not drinking alcohol is not enough for me*. I must stay involved with my church, Alcoholics Anonymous, and my sober friends; also, my sponsor to keep me in-check constantly. If I lose any of these, relapse is most certain to appear on my path of sobriety. It is important for me to listen and to accept all support in order to grow stronger and to make the changes needed in myself so I do not forget I have a disease that is called Alcoholism. It is cunning, baffling, and powerful. I do have the strength to defeat it and to live with myself joyfully and peacefully.

My first ten years of drinking were full of fun and I had everything going for me. Then one year, I found myself out-of-work and broke, and my relationships were being torn apart. In my late twenties, my body was addicted to alcohol and I knew it but I didn't care. For me to feel *normal*, I felt I needed to drink vodka or bourbon every moment I was awake. If I could not get it down, I would find a way, even sticking my fingers down my throat so I would throw-up, or eat lemons, olives, or salt. This led to ulcers but still I didn't care. When I had pancreatitis, I still drank as much as I could. Even the blackouts did not matter to me. My drinking has been so bad that when my doctor told me I may die, I didn't believe him. The horror of thinking about it all made me sick, but I still did not care. Even the DTs for a week at a time didn't stop me, for a pint of liquor would fix that right quick, I thought.

I have reached the point now that my body cannot handle it anymore. I end up in the emergency room every few months; my body has been damaged from drinking alcohol out-of-control like an insane person trying to kill himself. My eyesight, blood pressure, nerves, and anxiety levels have all been affected. I know the next step could be death; I have been close to it.

I drink for a month at a time and then I get sober for one month. I began working full time for North Star Tile and got sober but then they went bankrupt, they owed me thousands of dollars in back pay. I stayed sober for only one week, then drank for the next six months, and ended up in the hospital with pancreatitis, liver problems, etc. I again tried rehab for close to one year. I went to Set Free Ministries and let Jesus into my life. I stayed sober after that for another six months; then I started drinking because of my anger, rage, and disappointment in myself. This drunk lasted for several months and then I realized I must have Jesus and AA in my life 24/7.

"You will not find yourself by running from teacher to teacher, from book to book. You will not meet yourself through following any specialized method of meditation. Only by looking quietly within the self that you know can your own reality be experienced."

—Seth

Working The Steps

I was born in Chicago in 1945. My parents met in engineering school. When I was six months old, we moved to Paris where my father was assigned to help rebuild the French railroad system. I had a nurse who spoke English, French, and Yiddish; and so did I.

When I was just a three-year-old little girl, my mother died of polio. She was twenty-three and was seven months pregnant with my brother, who died with her. Daddy insisted on being transferred back to the United States so that his parents could care for me. I was moved from Paris to Iowa. My father's parents and sister were wonderful people, but they were strangers I had not seen since I was an infant. My father worked in Kansas City and came to visit on weekends. After my mother's body was shipped back from France, my dad and my mother's father had a terrible fight over the proper site for her grave. I never saw my grandfather again and didn't see my grandmother again until I was twenty-eight years old.

My father remarried when I was four years old. My stepmother and I disliked each other from the start. My parents continued to live in Kansas City and tried to begin a family. When my step-mom didn't get pregnant, she went to a doctor who told her she would never have a baby because of a "tipped uterus." After that discovery, my parents decided it was time for me to join them, they started me in school almost immediately because I could read.

My stepmother was unpredictable and violent at times. My father traveled at least four days a week and drank from the time he got home to the time he left on his next trip. He told me that if my mother was unhappy, it was my fault and he didn't want to hear about it. Sometimes, she would tell him stories about things I had done when he was gone; he would beat me. They sent me to Catholic school. I was an AD/HD kid before Attention Deficit Hyperactive Disorder was an official diagnosis. I drove the nuns crazy. I was asked not to come back to the Brownies after my first year.

I got drunk the first time when I was six years old. I sang a solo at a cousin's wedding and was rewarded with sips of champagne at the reception. I loved the feeling; I felt I was *enough*; pretty enough, talented enough, and thin enough. I got sips from adult's drinks every time I could after that.

By the age of nine, I had discovered that cough syrup with codeine was an excellent beverage and was easier to get than alcohol. It was available over-the-counter, and I "developed" a chronic cough. By the time I was eleven, my parents had cleared out everything in the medicine cabinet because I would take anything in an effort to get high. By thirteen years old, I had started dating and smoking cigarettes. My dad was my favorite drinking buddy. Wine was served at meals, as it was in France; mine was never watered. Daddy's intention was that I would learn to drink at home.

When I was fifteen years old, I had my first drug overdose on over-the-counter cold medicines. Some cold remedies contain belladonna as a drying agent; some pills had larger amounts than recommended and the high doses I took got me so high, I wandered around in a fuzzy dissociative state for three days. Later that week, I had my first blackout on gin gimlets. It didn't scare me. My father was hugely amused; my stepmother was livid; my boyfriend (who was twenty-one years old) was confused.

I graduated from high school at the age of seventeen and went away to college. I spent my freshman year drunk almost every night. I came home at the end of the academic year at eighteen years old, unmarried and pregnant. I wasn't too sure who the father was (thanks to my drinking) so I married the one who seemed the kindest. By that time, I averaged at least two blackouts a week.

My first husband and I lived in poverty for at least the first nine years of our marriage; so we drank mostly at my parents' house on weekends. I taught him to drink like my dad and me. My daughter was born five months after the wedding. I went to work in the printing business when she was nine months old. Once I started working, I felt entitled to drink more. By age twenty-one, I was blacking-out at least four nights a week. After a particularly nasty confrontation at work on a Friday, I came home and drank a fifth of Scotch in less than an hour. My husband, who worked the second shift and went to college, came home and found me passed out in bed. It didn't occur to him until I didn't wake up on Saturday that maybe this was worse than my usual drinking. I finally came to on Sunday. As soon as I could keep it down, I was drinking again.

During the course of the eighteen years I was with my first husband, we each acquired Bachelors and Masters Degrees. We had three children, a daughter, and two sons. We bought a home. We got out from our poverty. Most of our friends thought we had the "perfect marriage." Our children were charming and bright. He started his own consulting engineering firm. While I was in my last year of graduate school, he informed me he wanted a divorce. I read his journal and discovered he was having an affair with my dearest friend. I didn't tell him what I knew until after I had consulted an attorney.

My husband stayed with us for nine months while at the same time continued to see her. I finished my Masters Degree in counseling, took my comps and orals, and submitted my thesis. I didn't drink at home during that time because I was afraid that I would attack him in a blackout! He had been nagging me about my drinking for over fifteen years, so my new behavior confused him. I drank about every four to six weeks with friends during lunch or dinner during that period and didn't get drunk. I thought I was learning to drink socially.

The night he moved out, I decided to reward myself with a little wine with dinner and a scotch afterwards. The next morning, I came to after my first blackout in nine months and staggered to my daughter's door to get her up for school. She was seventeen years old and had come home from a date to find me passed out, again. She looked at me with utter contempt. I realized that my children could have died trying to save their drunken mother if there had been a fire. I knew I couldn't trust myself around alcohol and I felt that loss much more deeply than the loss of my husband. Later that day, her high school principal called to inform me she had been suspended for two weeks for selling "look-alikes" at school. ["Look-alikes" are pills that look like illegal substances.] I mastered my hangover enough to go to the school and pick her up. I smelled like a distillery.

Two weeks later, a colleague from graduate school called and said she had a job for me. My graduate assistantship expired when I finished my degree. She thought I would be perfect for a position in the addiction treatment center in the hospital where she was Director of Patient Services. I interviewed for the job and was hired! I started my training sitting in on groups. About a week after I started, the staff went to the Medical Director and told him I might not be drinking but I was an untreated alcoholic. He gave me the MAST test. I lied and scored 32 (8 would have been enough for a diagnosis of alcoholism). I asked my husband to take care of our children, then ages seven, eleven, and seventeen. I also asked him to sign for the insurance benefits for me and I entered treatment in the center where I had just been hired as a counselor.

The treatment center was a 12-Step based program. I was in treatment for twenty-one days. We all missed that I was also addicted to more than alcohol. By the time I completed the program, I knew I needed to go to meetings daily and get a sponsor who would guide me through the Steps. I went home to my barroom, my kitchen. There were painful memories in every room of the house. I started having panic attacks for the first time in my life. I had to face my children who were all furious that I had been gone and that their lifestyle was being reduced. We were living on my unemployment compensation and child/spousal support from their father. During this time, my daughter was deeply involved with a young man who was a "functional illiterate" and hung around with the local chapter of an outlaw motorcycle gang. Her younger brothers worshipped him however.

I went to AA meetings daily for the first six months I was sober, I worked the Steps. The fourth and fifth steps were terrifying the first time I went through them. I was afraid I would be told that I was too sick for AA. Instead, I felt understood and accepted for the first time in my life. I hung out with sober folk, some relative newcomers like myself and some with more time. My husband sued me for the custody of my children when I was four months sober, on the grounds that I was going to so many meetings that I must be neglecting them! They were in school full time and I went to noon meetings. The papers were filed but no hearing was scheduled.

My sponsor warned me about relationships in early sobriety. A friend, who was an attorney, asked me if I was married or divorced. I said, "Separated."

He said, "Non-responsive."

I was married. Nice married women from Kansas City don't date. I didn't. I discovered I had a moral compass after all.

Next, I discovered I had a spine. I began to assert myself with my children. It was clear to me that my daughter was already in active addiction. Consulting with my sponsor and the people in my support group, I knew that if I told her that she had to stop seeing her boyfriend, I would lose her. My sponsor told me that if I didn't do something about my family disease, I was going to drink again and die. I started going to Al-Anon.

At my first Al-Anon meeting, it was suggested that I needed a different type of meeting so I switched to ACOA (Adult Children of Alcoholics) meetings. I started trying to apply the Steps in ACOA to my relationships, especially my parents, who were both drinking, as well as my husband and daughter. My estranged husband didn't see anything wrong with the children other than they often didn't want to visit him. So, I didn't believe that I could successfully confront my daughter with what I believed about her, that she was an alcoholic. The Steps became even more important to me.

The treatment center where I worked closed when I was about two years sober and I went back on unemployment. I was out of work for another six months. Then I got a job at a treatment center in the same state but one hundred and fifty miles away. My daughter stayed behind when I left; the boys came with me. I knew, when I moved, that I had a job and my AA. It would be enough.

Working in the next treatment center, I suddenly saw that I had re-created my family-of-origin in my workplace. This treatment center was run like a dysfunctional, paternalistic family! My boys and I were barely above the poverty line. I learned to apply the Steps at work and to bloom where I was planted. Meanwhile, with my new insights and doing inventory work, I recognized I had re-created my family-of-origin in *every place I had ever worked*! I also recognized that I still had residual resentments and fear regarding my parents. More fourth and fifth Step work!

Then my father was diagnosed with lung cancer and died within eighteen months. My mother refused to allow me to attend his funeral which was twenty-five hundred miles away; I was devastated. My alternatives? Fall forward into a sea of booze and drugs and die; or, fall backward into the arms of my Fellowship. My sponsor arranged for a memorial service for my Dad at a local church and seventy-five AA and Al-Anon members showed up to help me put him to rest. We had an Irish wake (without the booze or corpse) at an AA clubhouse and I could believe he was at peace. Mother didn't speak to me for two and a half years.

By this time, I was sure that my older son was an addict. Also, my friends from my old home group were calling me to tell me that my daughter, who was living in her father's basement, was going downhill fast with her drug addiction. My estranged husband refused to participate in an intervention. He didn't see a problem. His attorney kept calling me for hearing dates on support issues, on custody, and on the divorce. I would take a day off work and the hearing would be cancelled. More Al-Anon Step work!

The woman my husband was living with, my old friend, was coming with him to pick up the boys for visitations. I usually avoided her and if she saw me, she looked terrified. I decided that if she was going to be their stepmother, she and I needed to be on good terms so I reached out to her, not as a friend, but as another person. We were able to talk respectfully but not intimately. A year later, she was diagnosed with brain cancer and died.

Then the police came to tell me that my son was about to be arrested. He was sixteen and had been involved with an older boy in a burglary ring. I intervened on him the next day and told him that he could enter treatment or face the courts on his own. On the way to the treatment center, I asked him about his younger brother. He said, "I've been using with him for years." At this time, he was only thirteen years old, I intervened on him two days later and he went to the same treatment center as his older brother.

By this time, I was five years sober with four years in Al-Anon. The boys came home from treatment and started going to meetings. My daughter, who had broken off with her ex boyfriend, saw herself in the eyes of another man and didn't like what she saw. She quit using, although she didn't go to meetings. She was hanging around with a young woman I used to sponsor.

Most of the sober teenagers and young adults in our area began hanging around at our house. Their families knew they were safe and sober, so they could stay as long as they wanted. One stayed for eleven years! The house was full, happy and noisy.

Then, my youngest son's left lung began to collapse. The first time, I was at work and he had hiked up the mountain behind our home. The teenager who was with him ran down the mountain to get help. His brother ran up the mountain after he called the ambulance to see what was wrong, then ran back down and called me. No one seemed to know why my son had this event but suspected it might be related to all the marijuana he had smoked from age six to thirteen! He was missing a lot of school; his grades began to slip. The school administration was unsympathetic. Because he had severe AD/HD, he was perceived as a troublemaker, and so was I. When I went to the school and objected to his suspensions, because he had missed too much school, I had medical documentation.

My older son did well in school for his final year and graduated. He went to work in a facility that served the profoundly disabled. His first love was music and he put in an application to the Musician's

Institute in Hollywood. He drove himself to Los Angeles in a car that I swore wouldn't get him across town. After a year in L.A., he applied to Berklee College in Boston. He presented his audition tape and was accepted. He completed his degree on student loans, asking me for as little help as possible. My daughter also started working as an aide in a nursing home for the indigent elderly. She married her boyfriend and decided she wanted to be a nurse and worked her way through nursing school.

Meanwhile, my youngest son continued to struggle. His left lung collapsed fourteen times and then his right lung also began to be affected. He dropped out of high school. He went to work at a garage where his hair sometimes froze to the floor under the vehicles he was working on. At that time, I referred to my marital status as "engaged to be divorced." I finally told my estranged husband that if he didn't get a different lawyer, we were never going to be divorced because his lawyer was bleeding him dry. He changed lawyers and we finally got divorced after six-plus years.

When I was seven years sober, I went to an AA service convention. I met a man named David who came from a different part of the state. We began dating, which meant he drove over three hundred miles one way each weekend to be with me and the boys. I consulted often with my sponsor and my support group about him. They said the relationship was apparently great for me; he said the same thing. After a year of long distance dating, he moved in with us, shortly before my oldest son moved to California.

I finally found another job and went to work for the state corrections system. I was hired to start an addictions treatment program. I did groups in English and Spanish for the next eleven years. During the three weeks I was in the training academy, my youngest son, then seventeen years old, was in charge of the house. That was fine for the first week; the second week, everything that could go wrong did! David was in the process of moving in with us so he and I were both there on weekends only. We all survived—the house, the kids, David, our pets, and all of the sober kids who called me Mom and hung around the house.

There was one complication to my new relationship which he told me on the day we met; David has a disease other than alcoholism that would probably shorten his life. He had inherited polycystic kidney disease (KD) from his mother's side of the family. His kidneys were already fully involved and were at least twice the normal size. He did not intend to go on dialysis or attempt a transplant. He was also a biker. He had spent a lot of his addiction on the fringes of society, although he had always been employed. Some of my friends found him intimidating. My family accepted him without reservation. We married after we lived together for about ten months. We rode to the wedding on his bike, accompanied by other members of our sober bike club. We rode back to our house where we celebrated with a combination of AA, Al-Anon, corrections coworkers, sober bikers, and the local outlaw bike club.

Six months later, David had a brain stem stroke. It was misdiagnosed as an inner ear infection and he was sent home from the ER on antibiotics and Antivert for the nausea. A month later, he was no better and I was talking to my sponsor almost daily about my anger over his lack of improvement. I had also started a private counseling practice and was working eight hours a day at the prison, as well as, another fourteen to twenty hours a week in private practice. I was attending at least three AA meetings per week and one Al-Anon.

David was lying on the couch, supervised by our dog, getting up periodically to vomit and then get some crushed ice. It wasn't that he was having a good time; he couldn't even read or watch TV. Because he couldn't keep food down, he lost twenty-five pounds in twenty-five days. But, he wasn't getting better. Our biker buddies would come and take him to meetings when he felt like it. Finally, his primary care physician requested a brain MRI which identified the area damaged by the stroke. It took another five or six months and a patient who was a Tai Chi teacher for David to begin to heal. I kept going to AA and Al-Anon just to keep sane.

After David regained his health, he went back to work as a drug and alcohol counselor in an outpatient treatment program. He finished his Masters Degree in rehabilitation counseling at a local Jesuit University. Eventually, he came to work at the same correctional facility where I worked. And one day, he told me he had changed his mind about dialysis which made me happy.

All my kids were succeeding at their careers and staying straight and sober. When I was eighteen years sober, my stepmother died suddenly. David and I, along with my daughter, went to California to take care of her final needs, arranging the funeral, seeing to probate of her will, and getting her condo ready for sale. I was able to close my practice at this time. Because of the Step work I had done on our relationship, I was at peace with her when she died. I had relieved her of the burden of my expectations and we did our relationship on her terms which was being intimate only to the level she could tolerate, not forcing her to the level I wanted. After all, I had my Fellowships to nurture me now.

David told me he didn't intend to spend another winter where we lived, in snow country. I said I wasn't moving without a job. I sent one Resume to the Betty Ford Center. I was interviewed via satellite and was offered a job! With the money I inherited from my family, we moved to California. The shift from state corrections was intense for me. David got a job at a different treatment center nearby.

Since that time, David has started working as a per diem counselor at the Betty Ford Center, in a different section from mine. The drama of the treatment center splashes and ebbs and then slows. My daughter and two sons all have given me wonderful grandchildren. They are all working in their chosen fields and seem to be reasonably happy with their lives. Yet, none of them is working in the field I would have predicted and each of them has married someone different than the person I might have thought they would have married. None of them goes to meetings. They all drink.

I have been sober for twenty-six years and have twenty-five years in Al-Anon. Almost as long as I drank, but not quite.

David started on his dialysis recently and says it is the most anticlimactic thing that has ever happened to him! Like any good dysfunctional family, none of the twenty-plus members of his family who have been dialyzed ever talked about it to him. His health has improved since he began his treatments and he is on disability now. I continue with the work I love. And most of all, I continue with my spiritual family which has carried me through things my family-of-origin would have carried me through if they could have; they just could not.

Thank God for 12-Step Recovery.

— Elaine

8   *Still Struggling*

Addiction is, in my opinion,
the problem of our time.

—Dr. Drew Pinsky

Not all addicts stay in, or even enter, recovery. Millions never try. It is estimated that only twenty percent of our addicted population succeeds in a complete recovery for life. Very sad statistic! When someone comes to a crossroads in their life, when they could choose sobriety, why would they continue to use?

The famous television addiction guru, Dr. Drew Pinsky (known as Dr. Drew) strongly affirms having an addiction is not a failure of willpower. Drew explains:

> "...there is a 'powerful biological explanation.' It has to do with neurological changes in the reward and survival system. Excessive drug use chemically tricks the brain so that the pursuit of the drug becomes a higher priority than survival."

Along with factors of genetic predisposition and the occurrences of childhood trauma, certain people just don't have much of a chance at living a straight sober life.

In an article from the "Addiction Treatment Forum" (Winter 2009), it states there is a memory connection when it comes to initial drug addiction and relapse. As research gains insight into the role memory plays in addiction, it may unveil why addicts can relapse decades after their last drug use. It is suggested that when "...vulnerable people feel the effects of an addictive drug, their brains may store that experience deep in the implicit-memory system." It has been noted by many people addicted to drugs or alcohol that they can crave the source long after they have stopped using it when they are reminded of it by environmental factors. Research has found this to be "...consistent with a process in which the brain's pleasure centers help addiction get started, but memory-like features maintain it over time."

This article continues to explore why an addiction haunts some, but not others:

> Why do some people become addicted, others not? Studies of identical twins indicate that as much as half of an individual's risk of becoming addicted to opioids or other drugs depends on genetic makeup. The other half of addiction-risk results from environmental factors such as external conditions, friends, family, and associates. If drugs are not available, a person with a genetic susceptibility cannot develop an addiction disorder. And someone who is not genetically predisposed may develop an addiction disorder if influenced by peer pressure to experiment repeatedly with an addicting drug.

It is difficult for many of us who have never experienced drug or alcohol addiction to grasp an addict's mindset. How can they allow their life to be so consumed? When they do abstain for a few months, a few years, how can they go back to their addiction knowing how hard it was to get straight and sober? No amount of questioning will settle our uneasiness and no amount of interrogating the addict will persuade them to stop.

One of the most important steps in dealing with your addicted loved one is to remember: each soul has its own destiny to fulfill. We cannot judge anyone's behavior but our own. We can only be responsible for our own life—actions, reactions, decisions, and choices. If an addicted loved one continues to use, it is not your fault; you are not to blame for their consequences.

One of my son's counselors in rehab told him when he returned after a relapse, "Rich, you made a 'reservation' with yourself that when you got a job or that long awaited relationship, or you made enough money, or bought a house—*then* you could drink." Rich confirmed this unconscious thinking with me. That's why he was back in another rehab facility. He was simply reasoning with himself that when he had it "together," he would be able to handle drinking again. It was his choice to put his decision to stay sober off for another time. It was his decision to choose to continue a path of pain, loss, and struggle.

We should not judge; the Universe does not judge. Spiritual teacher and author Gary Zukav writes in his profoundly enlightening book *The Seat of the Soul*:

> When you struggle with an addiction, you deal directly with the healing of your soul. You deal directly with the matter of your life. This is the work that is required to be done. As you face your deepest struggles, you reach for your highest goal... This is the work of evolution. It is the work that you were born to do.

Who of us can say that each addict is not living their ultimate life? Although their life appears to be filled with negativity and pain, who is to say their struggle is greater than our own? Each soul has a mission to accomplish, a lesson to be learned, which is the more privileged mission or lesson, yours or mine?

These next few stories are shared at the beginning of "breaking the silence." Each one holds the hope that by writing their words, their lives and habits would become self-acknowledged. One must put a name to a habit or pattern before taking the initial steps toward transformation.

The greater the desire of your soul to heal your addiction,
the greater will be the cost of keeping it.

—Gary Zukav

Wake and Bake

I have been addicted to marijuana, off and on, mostly on, for forty years which, I guess, makes me a drug addict. I smoke it almost every day, usually in the evenings when I have nothing to do to relax, as one would partake in having a glass of wine. I don't drink alcohol; on rare occasions, a glass of wine. As an older woman, my drug of choice is pot. I have a medical license to purchase it and to grow it, up to seven plants if I so choose. I choose not to grow right now. Anyway, I smoke such a small amount, maybe a hit or two a day. Sometimes, on a day off, I will take a couple of puffs in the morning as there is nothing better than a morning buzz, called "wake and bake" in the pothead world.

I do not really consider myself a drug addict or a "pothead" but I am addicted to pot and it is a drug; so if it quacks like a duck, then I guess I am. I can go several days without smoking without any repercussion, but that is usually when I am away from home and with other people. It is when I return to my solitary life that my pipe is always there waiting for me and beckoning me, like "Come on, you know you want to." I can never say no. And to make sure I never say no, I always have ample stash in my possession. I also have certain friends that like to smoke as well, and some family members. I am a highly responsible, intelligent adult and have many highly acclaimed accomplishments under my belt, and certificates and awards hanging on the wall of my office.

During the years in which I worked fulltime, I am now semi-retired, I never mixed the two, getting high and working. It was done solely on my time off. It was my comforting friend that I could always count on to make me feel better. Unfortunately through the many years of my drug addiction with marijuana, it did lead to other more serious drugs. That is something from my past, going back well over twenty-five years, and something I deeply regret. I got involved with the wrong people, made poor choices and flirted with many dangerous drugs, i.e. crystal meth, cocaine, crack, and all the psychedelic drugs in the late 1960s. What saved my life from the two most evil drugs of all, the meth and the crack cocaine, was my own inner spirit and self-determination.

One night, while being totally spaced-out on crack cocaine, I had an epiphany that I was selling my soul to the devil over this drug. And that if I didn't quit, I was going to lose my connection to God, to my Higher and pure Spirit, which was all about love and light and goodness. I was in the very depths of the darkest of hells and I wanted out. I wanted to be clean again. So I got clean and so did my partner at the time. We quit all the bad drugs cold turkey. We just did it! We compensated by continuing with our "safe" drug which is marijuana, and still do to this day.

— Anonymous

*If you are in the right intention, your story will bless
you and may be a blessing to many others.*

—Gail M. DeWitt

Still Numbing Out

I started drinking excessively at age twelve. My Dad received many gifts of booze from salespeople and stored it in the cellar. It was easy to steal booze as they really didn't maintain any inventory. Both of my parents were social drinkers. However, my Mother was a daily user of Darvocet and a very angry person. My father was timid, my two older brothers both "rageaholics" but not addicted to anything else but their rage.

As a boy growing up in the 1960s, a friend of mine went to Nam and sent me some powerful pot imported from Thailand. I started selling pot when I was sixteen years old, but was not a big smoker myself. I was really into amphetamines and alcohol more so, and then LSD, MDA, etc.

When I was 17, I crashed my car into a parked car and drove off; I got away with it. Then a neighborhood "pal" came by one night, and asked me to get him a glass of water, and introduced me to heroin. I chipped for years. [Chipping means periodical use of heroin] Not ever really strung out. But then I left Michigan for California and started shooting speedballs. [Speedballs, were cocaine and heroin, but in the last two or three decades speedballs can also mean methamphetamine and heroin] My veins were collapsed. I quit shooting dope.

Yet, when I returned to Michigan I started shooting up, blue morphine tabs and heroin again. Blood can only be drawn from my hands now. A blood test is a big deal and I always have to explain to the nurse to take it from my hand. I went back to Michigan and got involved in smuggling pot from Columbia. All the guys I grew up with were "in the business." Then cocaine came on the scene. We had plenty of cash and though not shooting it, we went through thousands of dollars getting high. Coke was a daily event, often times, three-day weekends without sleep. I had to take a lot of Valium to help with the crash. This was a major operation and daily overdrinking was the norm. I drove and drank with a pickup load of pot, like three hundred pounds of it! *Crazy.*

Eventually, the whole operation got busted. Why, after a Grand Jury investigation involving five states, I never got a knock on my door? I have no clue. Only two of us were not arrested. And yet, they knew everything about me. I thank God every day for the last twenty years for this miracle break from not going to jail.

I have never had a charge for dealing coke and pot. Then I stopped it all and sold real estate for awhile, worked for an airline, and finally became a clean and sober tour guide for the past twenty years. I have been luckier than most: many of my friends died of overdoses or car wrecks. In one car wreck, a friend was beheaded. A few were shot dead, a bullet in the back of the head, in bad drug business deals.

However, most of the people I was involved with were actually good people and reliable from my perspective. It was business and doing a lot of drugs. It was the "outsiders" who brought violence into the scene, not my childhood friends. They made "deals with the devil" and it cost some of them their lives.

At least five friends have committed suicide. One was looking at three to five years and decided to overdose rather than go to prison. One friend in federal prison watched someone get beaten to death over a blanket. All these stories come out of drug dealing and abusing drugs.

I am a survivor. Many others were not as lucky. I am still not sure what is God's will for me, but He has kept me alive and free and I still believe He has a mission for me to help others. I know I lack self-confidence; I can be very defensive, though less these last two years. I don't know if I will ever feel "good enough" or lovable. Mean people who project their unmet needs onto me send me in a downward spiral, no matter how kind and caring I am towards them.

No wonder I've been numbing out; I am still drinking. I can't deal with it. Like many, I just want to love and be loved.

— Lew S.

Man is a soul, not an institution;
His inner reforms alone can lend permanence to outer ones.
—Paramahansa Yogananda

Befriending a Higher Power

My story is not special. But I really think it's a story that needs to be shared. As I write this, I am a forty-nine year old man. I was an only child but adopted at birth. This is my addiction story and there are a lot of others out there.

My first memory of how ugly it could be was with my dad. Notice dad is with small letters. It's because I don't think he deserves to be capitalized. There was lots of alcohol. They weren't actually pouring it down our throats, but it was available. I've been drinking from a very young age. It was really just to be part of the crowd. I was sick as a dog the next day and they were just laughing at me. Mom used to say that a lot, "Calvin they aren't laughing with you, they are laughing at you." I just never wanted to believe that.

I was abused at a very young age. It wasn't some ugly story like you hear today, but I promise you it did a lot of damage. Today, I feel like I'm at the crossroads and I know an alcoholic beverage can't help me cross.

Another reason I drink and I know this to be, is living gay. I wasn't raised this way; yet, I turned out gay. I always felt like an outcast. I strongly believed what the Bible says about homosexuality; I'm always focused on going to hell for being gay. I'm not living; I'm just wasting a precious life.

I've been in three treatment centers and I also watched my father die of the complications from alcoholism. So, I have firsthand knowledge how alcohol kills. It destroys lives. I'm also living with full-blown AIDS. And it's by God's grace that I'm even able to communicate today.

I hope my words can help someone else. I strongly believe there's a reason I'm here. Maybe this is a start to make my star shine. That star part is about me being theatrical. I'm a somewhat actor. I was told that once and I got offended. But today I'm much better about dealing with what others say about me.

I finally got it today—it's about *me*. I am learning to do things differently. Not making the same old mistakes. I'm learning to take it one day at a time. I'm "Letting Go, And Letting God." I've learned all the things I've been through were to get me to where I am now.

Also, I know that I have a Higher Power I can lean on at all times. Just knowing this today is a much better high than alcohol or any illicit drugs. God can forgive anything; now it's time I forgive myself. I've been through a lot; drugs, sexual abuse, AIDS, and the loss of loved ones. But today I know it can only get better once I am clean and sober.

— Calvin N.

Let's be more creative, more open to change.
If something doesn't work,
let's not be so bound to continue with it.

—Mark W. Parrino

My Story (continued)

After nine years of living in our new home, doing what we could for Rich and his alcoholism, David was approaching the age when retirement sounded good. In 2004, we decided to move back up north near our daughter and grandson. This decision was rough for Rich—his enablers were moving away! Nevertheless, we did find a lovely gated-community in the country and settled into a life without the disruptions of a needy alcoholic son. We enjoyed almost two years before Richard appeared on our doorstep via the bus with nothing but his clothes in a bag and beer on his breath. My heart sank.

We pushed ahead with plans to help Rich yet again in this new setting. We motivated him to start a job hunt; to get applications for medical assistance; secure his driver's license reinstatement, and get some wheels. He did not stop drinking. Throughout that first year with us, he had several incidences of drunkenness and then he would self-detox to "try-on" sobriety yet again. We helped him find a place to rent in a trailer court twenty minutes away and coughed-up the first and last month's rental payments.

* * *

I just left the ER for the umpteenth time. I have lost track of the exact number of visits I have stood over my son's limp body lying in a hospital bed. As I walked into the room, I tried to intuit a faint aura around his still body to assure me he was alive. My heart broke yet again as I touched his sweaty brow with my cold hands from the winter night drive. When he felt my hands, he opened his eyes to meet mine. When my eyes met with his sad gaze, we instinctively shared a moment of love, of sadness, and of acknowledgment.

He had tubes and electrical leads attached to his body preventing much movement, but his walnut-colored eyes relayed his story. "This time," they said, "is the last time."

I tried to comfort him in my holistic-healing-way by holding his feet as they shook unwillingly. I closed my eyes and tried to imagine my Divine energy traveling up through his legs and into his still body, praying I was helping him to heal. The doctor arrived and informed me that while it was admirable that Rich had attempted to detox himself off alcohol, he was at a stage in his years of abuse that could not be stopped "cold turkey." This time Rich needed a medical detox program to alleviate the serious symptoms of withdrawal. He continued to say Rich had experienced *withdrawal seizures* and it was too dangerous for him to go through detoxification unsupervised.

Rich had learned his own form of detox many years ago whenever he decided to try, yet again, to become the sober man he so wished to be. Richard's magic detox regimen had become all too etched in my brain. He would start by making sure he had the necessary items required for several days of isolation while ridding his system of the poison that was consuming his life. He would buy lots of chicken broth, juices, and make sure he had plenty of water available. In addition, he would tell someone (usually me) that he would not be available for a few days. If there were pain relievers, Compazine suppositories, Valium, sleeping pills, vitamins and herbal teas available, all the better. He always assured me he would be fine.

I would wait for his call to come check on him. Usually I found him limp in a ball with pans at his bedside filled with vomit. But this time, even with all the "right detox stuff," Richard's body could not handle the dangers of withdrawal. Yes, at one point several years ago, when trying to detox himself, he experienced paranoid delusions thinking men outside his home were trying to kill him; and another time, he vomited so much his stomach formed bleeding ulcers. But, Rich had never experienced *seizures* while trying to detox, that I was aware of.

When I left the hospital this time, I felt I had lost a personal battle in being able to help my son overcome his alcohol addiction. After years of struggling to guide Rich toward his Light, I felt it was time to tell him I could no longer be the person to watch him slowly kill the Life Force trying so desperately to live within him.

I had made this decision many times, promising myself I would not become one of those clinging mother's enabling their addicted adult child. I knew this behavior was not healthy for either of us. After all, I am a counselor and knew all the heart-wrenching tales of parents with children they could not "get straight." Yet, I found myself becoming one of those parents. I learned quickly when Rich was drinking too much; when he should stop; when to coach him not to drive; when he was detoxing; and, rewarded him with hugs and praise when he stayed sober for a few months. I had become that enabling parent, as had my husband.

All the past years of living Richard's alcoholic drama rushed through my brain on that cold dark drive home from the hospital. I did not sleep that night, my blood pressure rose to deadly highs and my gut twisted inside. That night I detached my enabler-self from my being. I needed to go through my *own* withdrawals of allowing my alcoholic son to walk his chosen journey, wherever it might take him.

Rich's Story (continued)

The pain and misery that I suffer after each drink, kills me a little more each time. The hurt gets more intense. My realizing the hurt that I inflict onto everyone around me, especially my family, creates a guilt I no longer can handle by myself. My feelings are lost, my mind is numb to reality and my heart has hardened. With all of this, I should be spiritually dead; at one time not long ago, I was. I thank my Higher Power for the insight I have received in dealing with my disease and the acknowledgement that I cannot recover from it alone. My life is unmanageable; I am out-of-control. Alcohol rules over me. This must stop or I am going to end up dead if I get drunk one more time. I do not want to die a drunk.

I want back what I have lost in the years of my irresponsible behavior from drinking. This includes my family's respect and trust toward me in all matters of our lives. I want to be welcomed with open arms at family gatherings instead of the anger for what I have done to disrespect myself and them. Also, I want to be employed and hold a job without being fired every year or laid-off because I am too sick to go to work. I would like to become an asset to my employer, a valuable tool to the company.

I have lost a lot and I am determined to get all of it back, plus some. God willing...

9   *Difficult Lessons*

"I had to stand in another person's shoes and look at the world from that point of view. Whether people were homeless, closed-minded, politically motivated, or extremely wealthy, I had to slip into their skin and attempt to see life from their eyes."

—Atticus Finch

It is a fact that some addicts and alcoholics do not make it—they die. We don't usually hear or read a lot about those addicted to drugs or alcohol who have died with their addiction wrapped around them like a weight sinking to the bottom of the sea. Their stories cannot be told unless a loved one takes the time and has the insight to speak or write it down. There seems to be a type of shame attached to a story relating the death of an addicted person; people don't want to hear the details of what caused an addict's death. Why is this? There is no shame in death. Why should we shroud their lives in silence as if they never existed?

I feel the more we know about their life's tribulations, the more chances we have at finding solutions for others. It is all very pleasing to read and hear about success stories surrounding a happy ending of an addicted person making a choice to find his freedom and live a life of abstinence. Can it not also be of value to hear of those whose struggle was lost?

Again, I firmly believe each soul, each life, has a journey to unravel. Whether that journey is filled with wealth and fame or addiction and struggle is not the issue. The soul's journey is not lost if the physical body is gone due to choices which led him or her on a path of addiction. This journey is perhaps one of the most difficult for a soul and may be rewarded in some measure we can only contemplate. Who is to say one's soul journey through a life is of greater value than the next?

Every experience is a spiritual learning experience. Every path taken discloses a new level of teaching. Every soul has the free will to choose which path, which journey, to tread upon—this is our freedom of choice. Do not judge one soul because they left our material realm sooner than *you* thought they should. Our job is to find solace in their journey as a merit of willingness to try, once again, to walk among us.

Several years ago, I was fortunate to be in a few workshops with spiritual medium James Van Praagh, before he became world famous. He is a gentle man, standing barely over five feet tall with rounded face and twinkling blue eyes. His view of life and death set well with my own as I listened to his opinions and accepted his invitation to meditate with him. Van Praagh easily discusses his belief in souls and their journeys to learn, grow, and evolve through various lifetimes. He writes in his enlightening book *Unfinished Business*:

> "I agree that we do have a particular destiny, and we can either travel the more difficult path to it or veer off and do something completely different. It is our free will. However, this idea does not preclude our going through lessons, whether difficult or easy. After all, we have come to earth to expand our soul's understanding and grow to be great spirits; so lessons are a must."

It seems evident that some people with addictions choose to travel the difficult path, perhaps veering off from their true destiny. But then again, perhaps their true destiny was exactly the path chosen.

"Many spirits have told me that the Golden Rule is the doorway to human understanding.

They have said that if they could have seen others as themselves, their lives would have been less of a struggle, and they would have generated more love than hate."

—James Van Praagh

A Friend Gives Up

I would like to share with you the story of a very dear friend who is no longer with us. It is a story of addiction and much more. It is also a story of low self-esteem, self-abuse, and trying to find himself, trying to fit in. All this sent him seeking in the wrong direction and he ended up addicted to alcohol and drugs. But let me start at the beginning.

Johan and I were neighbors in junior high school and even though we were boy and girl, we became very good friends. We used to love the same type of music, same type of art, photography, and the same type of books, novels and poetry. Johan was a very talented young man. He wrote beautiful poetry, essays, and stories. I was more interested in drawing and painting. We finished high school together and went on to college; we graduated together. He remained in school to get his Masters degree; I went out and got a job working for Kodak.

A year later, I applied to work in television. We lived in South Africa, and at the time, 1975, we were getting television for the first time in our country. I was accepted and very quickly learned the ropes and got promoted to a director/producer. Johan decided to remain in school to receive his doctorate which he did four years after I first started to work. We remained close friends but I discovered that he was a closet homosexual. It didn't matter to me since he was my good friend.

Six months after receiving his Ph.D., he applied to the same TV network for which I worked. Johan traveled the six months between his graduation and starting to work in television, mostly in Europe and the United States. He loved America but he couldn't get a job here. Because of his writing talent, he was accepted in marketing and promotions. For a while, he was truly happy. He met up with talented people like him and he really thought he had found his niche both in a career and in his social life. During this time, I saw very little of my friend due to our work schedules and social life.

About six months into his new job as marketing and promotions Vice President, he invited me to go to a concert with him, I accepted. During an interval, I noticed that Johan was drinking a little excessively, in my opinion. Johan had never been into alcohol; he loved a little wine, but not hard liquor. But now that is what he was drinking, and drinking hard. On the way home, I realized he was drunk and we almost crashed into a street lamp pole. At first, I was angry and disappointed; and then, I decided that the time had come for me to distance myself somewhat from him.

Johan continued to socialize with his new friends and the shy, somewhat introvert, highly spiritual, beautiful being—that Johan was—turned into an alcoholic drug abuser and sexually promiscuous stranger. He befriended another homosexual and they used to spend nights in sexual orgies. Shortly after this, he started showing up for work totally inebriated both with alcohol and hard drugs. In less than eighteen months after he first started to work for television, he was dismissed. Johan lost his friends but his addiction did not abate. He refused to go for detox or help.

Although Johan earned a very good salary as a Vice President in his company, he had squandered it on his boyfriend, other sexual partners, alcohol, and drugs. So to be able to maintain his addictions, he accepted any type of job that he could find, which he subsequently would lose. This went on for quite a few years. By then, I had lost practically all contact with my old friend. I truly missed our time together, but Johan was not the same person I had known. I do understand that we all change as we grow. I tried to get him to seek help for his condition, but he became very angry to the point that he stopped talking to me altogether.

Then I immigrated to the United States and I had been here a couple of years when my sister let me know that Johan had contracted HIV. He was one of the first casualties of AIDS in South Africa. Instead of trying to change his life and seek help, he refused all support. He decided that he was going to go out with a bang. His addiction increased, his sexual promiscuity reached the level of debauchery, and he refused to take any medication. Johan, my brilliant, talented, and so very unhappy friend died of AIDS at the age of thirty-six. He left behind his parents who adored him and his sister. They thought that God had given them two incredible miracles in those children. You see, both his parents were deaf and Johan and his sister Martie were both unimpaired hearing people.

It was extremely hard for me to witness the self-destruction of my friend and not be able to do anything to help him; he just would not listen. It was almost as if he had a death wish. I am grateful that I was not there to see him suffer from AIDS. I was heartbroken. I don't know if I would have been able to watch him die slowly of this horrible disease.

Sometimes, I wonder what it is that can turn someone as beautiful spiritually as Johan was into a dark, desperately unhappy person who just gives up.

—Laura J.

However many holy words you read, however many you speak, what good will they do you if you do not act upon them?

—Gautama Buddha

My Story (continued)

After several false-starts, Rich began the new life he had always wanted. He did find that perfect job in which he was a great asset. He was a finish carpenter for a wonderful company who honored him and his struggle to stay in sobriety. He became motivated to enter an outpatient program for six months which began to turn his life around. He found a great little house to rent and new sober friends within a Celebrate Recovery® group. His life, as he turned forty-years old, finally looked positive and on track. I, of course, was proudly introducing him to my friends, taking him to lunch, meeting his new recovery buddies, and feeling very pleased and proud. Then he relapsed.

When I looked in his eyes, they were the lightest blue, like we imagine Jesus' to have been. Richard was not there, only a body void of soul, his walnut-colored eyes sucked out. I imagined an evil entity entering his drunken body snatching it up and claiming it for its own. I gripped his shoulders and shook them, shouting to his drawn sullen face, "Wake up! I know you're in there. Wake up and see your Light." He gazed in puzzlement at my useless attempt to rid his soul of the demon.

"We are done," I muttered not too loud but loud enough for Richard to hear. Three short succinct words that stabbed my heart as only a parent understands. I had heard these words over the phone, offered by a minister who was trying to soothe my distraught soul when a bell rang in my head.

"I might as well go get a rope and hang myself," he said in a fog-drenched depression which hung in his eyelids.

"I'll go with you. I've lived enough of this drunken life of yours," I retorted.

Of course, I didn't mean it—neither did he.

* * *

Richie's life took on many trials over the next several months. In 2008, he sustained a serious back injury, which caused him to go on state disability until he could recover from needed surgery. He fell through the cracks of the county's medical aid program and also he fell to his addiction once again. While waiting for six or seven months for his surgery consultation with the Orthospine Center at UCSF Medical Center, he found pain relief the old way, through alcohol. When we would check on him or arrive to drive him to physical therapy and other medical appointments, we usually found him rolled in a ball on the sofa, drooling the poison liquid which imprisoned him in a deep depression.

The end of the year came and went, leaving only memories of Rich's pain, drunken holidays, and anxious hope for the phone to ring signaling the specialist's orders for back surgery. With New Year's arrival, I took solace in the effort my son was demonstrating to sober-up in order to talk coherently and explain his condition to yet another doctor. The call never arrived; Rich continued drinking.

* * *

It has been raining for days now as I sit, lie, and wriggle in bed to find comfort. I developed shingles, a painful condition caused by stress which generates patches of a nerve-piercing rash around my waist. Stress—Rich wears it like a cloak that tosses smoldering embers when he turns abruptly to shout profanities while threatening to kill himself if we do not obey his commands. Even with all my holistic endeavors, I find stress cannot always be a controllable entity. It cannot be touched and thus moved to another space. It sweeps into the pores, into the cells, through the blood, and into the mind, settling there to torment its prey with worry and fear. My stress found its destination this time in the form of Shingles. Years ago, at the beginning of Richard's episodes of intolerant alcoholic rages, stress entered my intestines. They became a squirming snake eating at my insides.

Why have I allowed my son's rants of alcoholism to poison my body yet again?

I ponder this question as I open the window to hear and feel the wetness of the clouds touch my hand. I feel God close in my soul. The bamboo chimes sing their wood-song serenading my Quan Yin and Buddha, perched on opposite sides of deck railing. Two large creamy-pink quartz crystals lay quietly beside them soaking in the moisture as if to say "thank you" to each drop of promised rain as they assure my idols' safety.

Sometimes as a mother, I feel my duty is to keep myself at-the-ready for my two children. After all, I birthed them to life. When does a parent let the child slip into their own destiny?

The rain begins as I continue to stare out the window to receive an Oprah "Aha! moment." The cloud above releases the water from its grip, no longer willing to shield it beneath its soft breast; the moisture leaks out drop by drop, finding its own place among the earth. The landing may be soft like a blade of grass or an opening bud, or harsh splashing on a terror-filled patch of rock, hard and fierce. Even the fatherly Cottonwood branch cuddles each drop as it lingers for several minutes seeking shelter on bent limbs laden from winter. Without notice, as I glance up again, the drop of rain is gone, fallen to the ground to fend for itself.

Yes…I did the only thing a parent of an alcoholic can do—I let Richard fall to his destiny.

One reads much on "Letting Go" these days, the saying has almost become a bit archaic. I certainly repeated it thousands of times to my patients over the years. An adjunct phase is "Let go, Let God." Does one really understand the concept of allowing Something More, God/Goddess/All That Is, to take over an unsolvable issue? As I looked for answers in the many books alluding to this action, I found a few treasures then made my own to hold in my heart for solace:

> Letting go is the Action part of Faith
> To let go is not to Deny, rather to Accept
> To let go is not to Judge,
> But to allow another to be a human being

> *Suffering is in the mind. How we perceive happiness determines our suffering or not.*
> —His Holiness The Dalai Lama

Life is a process. Not good, not bad, only a process. Some people follow the rules they learned early in life only to find themselves in despair and pain. Others try-on new concepts and beliefs challenging their very existence and choose higher roads to explore. We all make our decisions based upon what we have learned in childhood and who we perceive ourselves to be. This Divine gift given to us all is called *freedom of choice*. It is imperative that our younger generations grow to understand this power of choice and that it is their doorway to life. We can foster a sense of freedom within them just by sharing our own stories. Whether enlightened stories or darkened tales, our stories will give them the freedom to unfold their choices to compose their own life stories.

There are hundreds of good books on the shelves of libraries and bookstores which can help guide our children toward a life without addiction. Perhaps it is the right time to bring one home and share it with your children. The more we talk about our fears and pain that surround the topic of addiction, the more we are giving of our Self, which is exactly what every child desires. To give of our Self, we must leave the suffering behind and reach for the positive side of life. Sharing joy, love, and compassion with our younger generation instills a sense of internal spiritual freedom they will readily grasp.

I was honored to attend a teaching seminar by His Holiness The Dalai Lama in 2004. It was presented in a small auditorium, so I was able to really feel his energy and see the expressions on his peaceful face. Upon entering, my eyes fell instantly to the stage with its decorations in honor of the Buddhist tradition. There was a row of hundreds of white candles glowing along the back, evenly spread from one end of the stage to the other. Hanging directly over the row of candles were three huge tapestries with images of Tara (the Tibetan Kuan Yin), The Buddha, and one other figure I did not recognize, perhaps Bodhisattva Nagarjuna since his lessons were to be studied in this seminar.

On the center stage was a magnificent golden statute of The Buddha sitting high on a platform; it must have been seven feet tall. In front of The Buddha was a structure for The Dalai Lama, six or seven stairs leading to a comfortable sitting-pillow, capturing a dark red carpet. There was a small table or shelf on the left for the sacred tablets of teaching instruction from which His Holiness would so gently handle as if they were his precious children. The tablets looked as if they were made of cherished light wood or heavy parchment paper. Each one fit together in a golden yellow cloth with a tie that wrapped around them tightly to secure their sacred contents. Each time the Dalai Lama came into the room, he was given the cloth to unfold exposing the tablets for their instruction. Then, before he left the stage, he carefully tucked them in again, personally wrapping and tying them lovingly together. Just in front of the seating structure for the Dalai Lama were two great bouquets of Calla Lilies, my favorite flowers.

On both sides of the platform where the Dalai Lama reigned, sitting for hours crossed-legged, sat his disciples and monks. There must have been two dozen or more. They were donned in their finest of cloths and robes wrapped respectfully in the Buddhist's tradition of respect. The robes were colorful in bright oranges and reds, just a few had chosen white; it was unknown to me as to the meaning of these colors. Later, I was told by a student that these colors represented the planting and harvest seasons in Buddhism. Most of the monks had shaven heads, wore sandals, and a few carried prayer beads or prayer wheels. They sat in silence the entire time, except for the very beginning of each morning's teaching. At this time, they performed a most magnificent chanting mantra that made my spirit soar to the very heights of the domed ceiling!

The outstanding interpreter sat close to the edge of the center stage with a small table which held a microphone and a few pieces of paper on which to write his notes as the Dalai Lama spoke. Not knowing whether Tibetan or Chinese language was being translated, it seemed to me this translator did an unbelievable job of getting each and every word spoken just as directed. Only a few times did the Dalai Lama interrupt him to either correct or add to what he was saying. At these times, it was as if to make sure we, the audience and students, totally understood what was being taught.

What was said? What words of wisdom did His Holiness share with us? I have my notes; I have the thirty page booklet printed by the Buddhist Association that brought him here for this one time visit to the United States for the year. But the teaching, for me, came from inside like a blossoming of ripe fruit spreading within me as he spoke in a translucent tone. He spoke of suffering, "We create causes that give rise to suffering." He spoke of transformation, "Walk with the Nature of Reality when creating transformation." And, he spoke of intention, "The *intention* of what you do and say is what matters, not the act itself."

I watched and felt the love in the large auditorium illuminate and fill each person with understanding that needed no words. I witnessed many in the audience sitting cross-legged with eyes closed for hours. The foreign words came to my ears as His Holiness spoke and brought a sense of aliveness that I had not experienced. The words in translation entered my mind but did not find a permanence that would endure my repeating detailed meaning, and my mind wandered as my soul left my body to places unnamed.

I don't know what I expected to witness when I decided to attend this seminar; however, every minute in the presence of this truly Holy Soul was such a gift that I will treasure the experience my entire life. The philosophical teachings were on a level far above my understanding but I know the few words of wisdom I did retain feel like jewels within my heart. Being in the company of The Dalai Lama and seeing his smile with slight embarrassment and a quick apology, as he picked-up an orange sun-visor cap to shield his eyes from the glaring stage lights, will always be the memory of this day that makes my own lips part from ear to ear.

In whatever spiritual endeavor we experience, and share with our children, there are words of wisdom to guide us if we choose to find them. His Holiness The Dalai Lama said, "We must knead our minds skillfully, and with patience and perseverance we shall find that *our concern for the well-being of others will grow*." He said there is no secret to giving loving-kindness; it is called compassion. To be compassionate is to love others, as well as ourselves. This one lesson, if *only* this one lesson, is passed to our younger generations, we can succeed in helping our addicted population toward their wholeness.

My Story (continued)

My husband's name means Beloved; he is mine. I feel safe when he is home, in peace when he is away. There are more glances between us now than words. We read together separately. His books are of sports and Bibles, mine psychology and metaphysics. Separately together we read. Separately together we live as the two tall pines on our hill named after the many deer which roam up and down finding grassy bush along their daily journey. As the two pine trees, we sway in the wind, sometimes touching, sometimes stretching apart, but always firm in the soil we have rooted together.

Richard's journey through alcohol has also taken a painful yet unseen toll from his Dad. His hopes and dreams of his son finding his way to sobriety are long-lived. Now, his last attempt to hold tight the reins is over. He too understands his son must live his own choices, not ours. One morning, David held me tight in bed, not too tight to disturb my Shingle-inflamed body, and let me cry. At that moment, he became my "soft shoulder" which Dr. Phil repeatedly proclaims our partners should be.

The lake is cold to the touch and green to the eye. Winter drapes its sullen face to shroud it in layers of silt and sediment. In our yard, there is a birch tree. Its white trunk glistens in the rain as its arms droop with weight as if the little drops are holding them down. It bends to the ground like a willow. I have always loved willow trees. This day, I feel like a willow looks.

Our friends leave gifts of food for us. They intuit that my Shingles are limiting my cooking abilities; they are right. Such love is welcome. I asked if they would continue their gifts of foodstuff when my Shingles have healed; we laughed and one said, "You betchya!" with her best Sarah Palin smile. In my book *Gifts From the Child Within*, I wrote about re-creating the past. Perhaps in the future, I will remember to re-create this present.

I sit. I listen to the echoes of the CD spinning lightly as the rain makes its journey downward. The bamboo flute chirps its notes in a rhythmic ritual with an occasional Chinese gong shattering the cadence as though to address its presence. I love to sit and listen to meditative sounds as I write or read or think. Filling my cells with renewable energy, the music pushes my shoulders down and my chest breaths deep again. Even our dog Goldie lies still, at rest, her eyes rolling in their lids as she drifts to the silencing sounds. I squirm as a picture of my son haunts my mind finding him in a gutter drenched with mud and rain and frost. My Shingle-hives reach up and grab me at my sides turning my nerves into jolts of spasm. "Let go!" I shout at them then softly laugh at the double meaning.

* * *

It has been six days since the delusional rampage which forced us to place Richard's personal belongings neatly on the porch after he left for work. He has left several messages on my cell phone with deep apology, his voice strained with the fear that we will never answer. As I listen, my heart turns over and thumps out loud. He reports he is trying to find a bed in a rehab center. Will he say he needs to see us? Will he ask forgiveness for his unacceptable behavior, profanity, and threats? Is his back pain bearable? Is he still drinking? My thoughts rage with animalism for what he has put us through again.

Years ago in college, I read about the "elephant in the living room syndrome" which the addict declares. I knew and agreed to this aphorism; I lived it in my childhood. Our entire family revolved around my father's alcoholic whims of traveling across the United States every few years, trying to find peace for his inner child's broken heart. I lived his tortured life for eighteen years; for this past eighteen, I have lived my son's.

When parents know their child is near or at hitting their *rock-bottom*, it tests every dream and conviction they hold. Only questions confront us now. Do we help? How? Do we tell him he is not welcome here? Do we allow him in our home to use the phone, the toilet? Do we give him food? Do we drive him to his church and drop him off on the steps? Do we help make calls to more rehab centers?

We are sadly familiar with these questions having experienced this scenario several times. But this time is different; we had said "We are done"—we had not before. This time the mind-questions do not seem so urgent. No longer able to worry where he sleeps or how he gets his food, I leave those thoughts un-addressed. I will not allow Richard to enter our home again to fall forgotten on the floor in his passed-out coma.

> *Life is lived in the small places, the in-between spots*
> *whose magic lies in their capacity to reconnect us to our*
> *souls.*
>
> —Joan Borysenko

My Story (continued)

Rich is homeless, jobless, foodless, vehicleless, and penniless. Perhaps sober, as he tells me on the phone, but trust will appear only in the months ahead. He is applying for food stamps, money stamps, bus stamps, medical stamps, and whatever else he can at the Social Services Department. As much as I want to step in and help, each breath assures me what we are *not* doing is the beginning of Richard's *doing.*

Sleeping more comfortably now, I wrap myself up tight in a white down-coverlet looking like my favorite flower, the Calla Lily, with my blond-gray stamen head peeping out. When I turn gently on my side, the amulet with its etched *OM* symbol, signifying Universal Love, falls at my fingertips. I purchased one for my daughter and one for myself several years ago, neither of us removing it since. The gold shaped teardrop is cool and gives me comfort as I pray for safety and direction for Rich and strength for myself. I finger the familiar gem and drift beyond thinking.

* * *

David's Bishop came to counsel us last night. What a gentle soul he is. Sitting across from us, quietly listening to our tale of an alcoholic son, his eyes begin to water and he removes a tissue from his jacket's inner pocket. As I relate the years past, it sounds so repetitious, almost mundane to the point I pause and want to say "yada yada yada" but realize that would sound uncaring; so I continue, then finish and wait for a response. The Bishop begins his counseling with support for what we have gone through and how we have been able to keep ourselves from getting any more ill than we were.

He talks of others he knows who have family members with similar addiction stories and suggests we take a trip to get away. Then he brings up the topic of young adults and their "badge of entitlement" which they wear so openly these days. I realize David can use these words; to cement them in his mind will allow him to let go just a bit more of our son's unreasonable demands and alcoholic life. The dynamics of the Entitlement Syndrome is all too familiar to me.

The next morning is a damp mix of showers and fog; Rich calls from his night's bed under a bridge near our home. His voice rough and dry, I hear the familiar vodka drawl within his few words about not finding a rehab center which make my stomach lurch and my ears go deaf. I pass the phone to his Dad.

* * *

I am cold as I draw myself deep into my familiar Lily. I have taken all the necessary sleep aides to dull my Shingles pain and close my eyes only to hear myself moan, then realize it came from my husband's fitful slumber. At least Richard had agreed to enter a rehabilitation center, but calling the list given him by his recovery program resulted in "No beds available."

David decided to pick Richard up and drop him off in a trailer park to stay with a friend Rich had met while living there. Rich will need to wait to discover if he again meets with the seizures of his withdrawal. His doctor gave him a prescription for Valium to help ward-off the deadly convulsions while detoxing. I twist inside, feeling a bit of guilty relief that I will not have the ER watch this night. I get up and take another pill silently wishing my mind-rummage would cease and allow sleep's healing to cover my body.

I talk daily to relate the day's Richie-saga to family and special friends trying to hold my tears back. I ask them, "Don't all the homeless people and overly-full rehab centers and shelters throughout our country speak loud enough for society to hear the cries of our needy addicted population?" Addicts seem to tick-out some rhythmic tune which keeps them alive when all the odds say they should be dead. I know not all addicts do survive, but with 22.3 million adults in our nation living with addiction and another 20 million in recovery, many do. They must have something inside their brains that signal survival, not defeat, as they fight against the dying of their Light.

The cloak of sleep is upon me now as I dream in the silence searching for truth. Truth tiptoes in without our notice to light upon the senses of emotion and knowing. Learning to watch for it during times of reflection or meditation can be daunting; for if we acknowledge we are waiting for it to drift into our reality, it will not arrive. But instead, we must be silent without expectation, then Truth will visit us.

* * *

I awoke with tears in my eyes, remembering the dream which entered my sleep just moments before. It was a flying dream, the kind I like best...

I was visiting my sister's house five hundred miles away. The whole family was gathering, getting ready to go on a trip together and they decided to spend the first night there, each family in all their prospective RVs and trailers. This is something we all like to do a few times a year, traveling to the desert to ride dirt bikes or the dunes at Pismo Beach. I realized there was nowhere for me to sleep, but that David and Richie were inside our daughter and her husband's RV with our grandson. Since I didn't feel like sleeping anyway, I went to find Cayley, my four year old grandniece. She was waiting to dance with me. Her tiny feet perched atop my own as we glided in the air above all who slept.

The following day, my sister came outside and announced to everyone that someone had died. I couldn't hear what she was saying. Everyone began talking softly and the trip was canceled. They hung a large banner at the eaves of the house, declaring a death in the family and the memorial date.

Next, I found myself at the funeral, lying very still as I watched all the people arrive; so many came. The service was outside and as each person arrived, they were given three of my books to take to their seat. I knew I was awake, but I also knew I needed to keep my eyes closed and be very still. I listened to everyone talk about my writing, but I didn't understand why they all were talking so much about it, and me. I heard wonderful comments and words like "poetry" and "genius." Lines and sentences from within my books were being read aloud by all my family and friends, both alive and those in spirit-form.

I continued lying silently still, not to interrupt, my eyes closed and crying inside with gratitude for all their praise. Then everyone's words hushed as a few people came upfront; I wanted to peek to see who it was but knew I should not. It became deathly quiet and I decided to walk over to the little path on the other side of all the people, so I stepped out of my body and left in search of the path.

I found it and it led to a beautiful scene of sandy dunes leading to the ocean below. Two rainbow trout were flying in the air and below the bluff two coyotes began hunting. I got a bit nervous then and turned to go back. The coyotes ran after two gazelle and downed them. There was one rabbit and little creatures all around me. I followed the path back to the funeral and found the people singing hymns and I began to cry. As I watched and walked past them, they nodded at me without interrupting their song, and I continued to the opposite side where there was another path.

I awoke with tears in my eyes, remembering the dream which entered my sleep just moments before and a glint of the morning sun etched across my bed and kissed my face. Lying there for another half hour, I reflected on this dream and what my inner guides were trying so desperately to tell me. Then I sat up, reached for my dream journal, and began writing it out in detail before the memory slipped away. These are some of the jewels I discovered from within this dream:

I do not want to die yet.
I will not allow Richard's drama to kill me.
I am loved so much more than I know.

Knowing how important all the details of a dream are to grasp its unfolding significance, I searched the Native American spiritual tradition of understanding the lessons which the animals around us can teach. I found the Coyote is called the Medicine Dog. My husband and I actually saw our first coyote strutting up Deer Hill just a few days ago and looking quite lost. He is a sacred animal, proud of his ability to trick others. Here is a quote about the Coyote from the Medicine Cards:

...you may not be conscious of your own pathway of foolishness. You may have conned yourself, your family, your friends, or even the public at large into believing that you know what you are doing. But listen, Coyote. You are balled-up in your own machinations. You have created a befuddling, bewildering, confounding trick. Pick up the juggler eyes from the ground and put them back in their sockets. See through the genius of your acts of self-sabotage.

Obviously, Coyote Medicine came to both heal my Shingles and my self-pity!

I also looked up what Rabbit Energy meant and found that it

represents Fear. The passage reads: *Sacred little Rabbit... Please drop your fright! Running doesn't stop the pain, Or turn the dark to light.* Very self-explanatory.

The two gazelle in the dream are not mentioned in Native American nature because they are not from our nation; so I looked in my good 'ole Webster's and found: *Any of various small antelopes... noted for graceful movements and lustrous eyes.* I consulted my trusty Medicine Cards once again and there was the Antelope. The words swirled in my brain as I read them aloud, learning why I had dreamed the Antelope Medicine:

> Antelope signifies knowledgeable action... Looking at Antelope, you become aware of your mortality and the short time span you have on this planet. With this in mind, you must act accordingly. Proper action pleases the Great Mystery. Antelope medicine is the knowledge of life's circle. Knowing of death, Antelope can truly live. Action is the key and essence of living.
>
> ...If you are balled-up and twisted in knots, antelope powers will speak to you of proper action and soon set you free...Listen and, even more importantly, act.
>
> ...Always listen to what antelope has to say to you. Antelope in your cards [life] indicates a message of higher purpose. Antelope arms you with the Bow of Authority, and forces you to act on behalf of self, family, clan, nation, and finally, Mother Earth. Antelope says, "Do it now. Don't wait any longer." Antelope knows the way, and so do you. Take courage and leap; your sense of timing is perfect. When Antelope has bounded into your [life], the time is now. The power is you.

Wow! This dream rocked my very being. In my dream, I took the *other path*. I will not stay in this cloud of depression a minute longer. I have books to write, people to meet, and places to visit.

The significance of the number *two*, which showed itself numerous times in the dream, represents my over-sensitivity to others. In numerology, the number two is the challenge of being too thinned-skinned, too easily hurt. My favorite Numerologist, Christine DeLorey, writes that the number two energy needs to:

> ...admit that you are, indeed, a very sensitive person...You must admit that you try to do too much for other people and

then become exhausted by your efforts. You must admit that you are not super-human and there is only so much of yourself that you can comfortably give to others.

You must understand that two is the number of intuition—the ability to sense. And the talents involved are heightened awareness, diplomacy, peace-making, and detail orientation. Just imagine how many ways you can use these skills to improve not only your own life, but also the lives of other people. And because you are able to sense all sides of a story, your ability to create peace from chaos is immense. You can also make yourself indispensable to others by exposing important details they tend to ignore.

Also in the dream, the number *three* was presented as three of my five books being read by those at the memorial service. The number *three* symbolizes the Divine Trinity. I am not sure what the fish represent, but my chosen logo is of two Koi fish juxtaposed with each other as if to signify the balance of the Yin/Yang or female/male energy. I have this Chinese artwork hanging in my home.

I answered Rich's phone call today. He said, "Please forgive me."

I said, "I already have." He shared his last attempts to find a bed in a nearby rehab program—there were none available.

10 From Chaos to Clarity

"There is no need to run outside for better seeing, nor to peer from a window. Rather, abide at the center of your being; for the more you leave it, the less you learn.

Search your heart and see if he is wise who takes each turn: The way to do is to be."

—Lao Tzu

Being in the present is not easy; being in the present is a personal experiment. How many times do we go into our soul's center and sit? The great masters of the world relate to us the benefits of meditating regularly to connect with our Self. This is a difficult task in our world today with all its hustle and fast-paced energy directing us to strive yet further into the unknown realms of science, social issues, metaphysics, and medical breakthroughs. To sit and savor the noise, smell, and sights around us is not a likely answer to be received by those climbing their success ladders.

As I write this sentence, I hear the leaves in the tree outside my window rustling; the bird in the distance chirping his rhythmic tune; the wooden chimes at my front door welcoming a light breeze signaling nature's call; and a slight bark of a neighbor's dog. Just to take a few minutes to delve into my being is a delight I cherish. As we ponder our lives and our choices, we sometimes find regrets, sometimes satisfactions, but to stay too long with either will not bring us peace.

While being in the moment within your thoughts and nature around you, focusing on important issues with that hint of spiritual knowingness which comes in its individual appearance, can bring rewards of gratitude, self-love, and hoped-for direction. When chaos is knocking at the door, pull up a chair, close your eyes, take a deep breath, and sit.

Do you have the patience to wait 'til your mind settles and the water is clear? Can you remain unmoving 'til the right action arises by itself?

—Lao Tzu

My Journal

I feel like I have been a sequestered juror locked in my house, instructed to listen carefully to all the voices in my head relate their opinions about what I need to do, or not do. Looking up, I see *seven* deer grazing together on the hill today; their heads intermittently bob up to check for danger. Their ears are long and perk to hear each noise and flicker imaginary flies. My husband likes to give them fruit and vegetables to eat and an occasional slice of stale bread. We know we shouldn't, but do it anyway just to assure their return.

The number seven is my favorite number. I picked it when I was a young girl. I liked to write it out to watch the flow from top to bottom in one smooth mark. I like to use the notch at the top but not the slash across its middle as some do. It has been a lucky number for me, although I cannot recall just how or when, I just know it. So the seven deer, I tell myself, have come to visit me to bring me luck. In numerology, the number seven represents the life challenges of Faith, Trust, Intuition, and Knowledge. No wonder my younger-self instinctively chose this number to help guide my life journey.

I check my numerology religiously, searching the words for clarity and meaning. Here are a few of the readings from these past traumatic months:

...Be prepared to learn new things as the situation changes. Some changes will occur of their own accord. Other changes must be made by you. One small change will lead to another—opening up an entirely new direction for you. We are all afraid of change. When fear arises this month, allow yourself to feel it, instead of pretending that you're not afraid. Acceptance of your feelings will provide the answers you need. You will then be able to proceed intelligently and confidently.

...Endings must now be made in a way that will allow you to walk away from a certain situation without regret. Be patient, tolerant, open minded, forgiving, compassionate, and optimistic. Above all, accept and enjoy the feeling that is urging you to believe in yourself... Situations may arise which test your patience and tolerance.

...This cycle will also teach you a lot about giving—and that giving and receiving are equal parts of the same process, as one cannot be achieved without the other. There are so many ways to give: your time, support, money, service, understanding, sympathy, creativity. But giving out is not the only way to give. Sometimes giving involves giving in, giving way, or even giving up.

"Almost anybody can learn to think or believe or know, but not a single human being can be taught to be. Why? Because whenever you think or you believe or you know, you are a lot of other people, but the moment you are being, you are nobody-but-yourself.

"To be nobody-but-yourself in a world which is doing its best night and day to make you everybody else, means to fight the hardest battle which any human being can fight, and never stop fighting."

—E. E. Cummings

Was I giving up on Richard? What about my song, "Don't Give Up?" When questions seem to roam my mind day and night without an end in sight, I believe it is best to sit in silence and listen. Listening to the silence deep within or dreaming in unawareness is always better for me than trying to tell myself logically what I need to do. Another method of receiving guidance from within to reach that Something More is using divination tools such as spiritual decks of insight and healing cards like the Angel or Meditation Cards.

My husband and I have a sacred ritual of pulling Rune stones and picking Native American Medicine Cards at the start of each year. We had not thought to do this at our usual time, the first day of the New Year, due to the Richie-drama consuming our days and nights. Today, David suggested, "Let's pull our stones and cards!" Even though it was late January, we felt excited about receiving a little guidance and direction in our trauma-filled lives.

David's animal totem cards were both ocean dwellers, which seemed to fit this year for him. They instructed him to confront and express his emotions which are buried deep—water represents emotion. The first card was the Whale energy asking him to release stored records (emotions) using "... your voice to open your memory... so that you may further explore your soul's history." This seemed appropriate advice. Next, he turned over the Dolphin energy card which represents "manna" or Life Force. This card instructed David "...to link with the Great Spirit and bring answers to your own questions or to those of others. " This was a monumental challenge for my husband because he is a quiet minimal-communicator, speaking only when necessary. *It will be interesting to watch if he takes on the Dolphin challenge this year.*

Then David carefully placed his fingers in the soft purple pouch housing our precious Rune stones. They are actually made of clear quartz crystal, a gift I gave myself several years ago after receiving a bag of regular plaster stones from a dear friend in the late 1980s. I have used the sacred Oracle of Runes hundreds of times with my patients during counseling sessions with an undeniably positive response. My husband's hand appeared from within the pouch, holding the customary three stones to be laid out in the sequential fashion. We bent over them as if they were bringing us long lost information we already knew but needed to remember.

The Runes explained that, for the year 2009, David was to be in a state of "non-action" and wait for inner growth to show him the way; to wait for messages, signals, because of his lack of clarity or awareness in a situation; and, that he may feel blocked and it is time to be clear with himself. The stones conveyed, "No matter what area of your life is in disarray, stop and consider: You will recognize the outer enemy as but a reflection of what you have not, until now, been able or willing to recognize as coming from within." Very clear advice.

My own Medicine Card animals were so vivid in my recent dream that I did not pick cards, but related to David the details of the power animals which had appeared to me. The Runes were also very supportive of my "Wake-up!" dream, as well as, indicating movement for me this year. "A relationship may need to undergo changes if it is to live and grow." Also, they instructed me to be in my defense mode while flowing with what life unfolds, "...The ability to foresee consequences before you act is a mark of the profound person." We both felt less heavy after performing our yearly ritual together.

Some of us live and some of us die
Someday God's going to tell us why
Open your heart and grow with what life sends
We'll meet again at the festival of friends
                                        —Bruce Cockburn

I have never experienced a day passing as slowly as February 23, 2009. Sitting in my home office, talking on the telephone to a dear friend who lives seven hundred miles away, we were laughing at something I don't remember when David's car drove up the driveway. He had gone to check on and ask Rich if any of the rehab beds were available yet. Rich was still visiting with the friend in the trailer court who lived near the large lake where they fished for bass.

While still chatting on the phone, David came into the room and stood directly in my vision so I would see his hand motion across his neck to "cut off" the conversation. His face was stark and he was shaking. Instantly, I told my friend I needed to hang up; she instinctively understood the tone of my voice and said her good-byes.

I looked up at my dear husband's white lips as my hearing failed me when he began to speak.

"What?" I mumbled not wanting to hear the words a second time.

"Richie died," he said succinctly. No second guessing, nothing more to hear.

My brain and heart didn't understand as I motioned for him to sit down in a chair as my sobs rose from deep within my soul. That day, each minute was an hour; each hour became a day, as time seemed to stop.

Our son was dead. Our son is dead.

* * *

The next day my raw voice answered the phone, knowing I would need to relate the events of the day before to more relatives. A cheery man's voice stated he was from one of the rehabilitation facilities Rich had contacted—they now had a bed for him. Through my sobs, I told the man Rich had passed-away the day before. He was very sorry and saddened that he was a day late.

The cards, flowers, and plants keep arriving. In appreciation, I pen thank you notes. I stare out the window not seeing as words of loss, grief, and sympathy seem to pass through me like shooting stars on a dark black night. The memorial service was perfect. The hugs were truly accepted. The food I am sure was offered in delicious abundance, although I don't remember eating any of it. I do remember many of the heartfelt words from friends and relatives who spoke in the chapel or sent their sympathies to us in honor of Richard, here are just a few:

My heart is broken...my big brother is gone. What will I do without you Richie? I miss you so much already. I am shaking with sadness, my chest hurts, my soul feels empty because I will not see your smile with my eyes again or hug your big chest. You are my match, you are the only other one like me. You are my brother and no one else knows me the way you do. You are my other-half of our family.

Rich was the best employee we ever had....

Richie had a naturally friendly smile that came from within his heart. Too friendly for this hard, tough world. Yet, it's just what this world needs more of... friendly people. You knew him better than anyone. Yet everyone that knew him, knew him as a friend who had their best interest at heart. I am glad I knew him. I can remember many conversations I had with him; never a mean word ever came from his mouth. His speech was honest and upright, the overflow of his heart.

Rich was a great kid that made me smile a lot and grew into a special man. You two were blessed to have him as your son and Richie was truly blessed to have the two of you as parents.

I want to say to you both that there are not many human beings who are afflicted with alcoholism addiction that have the opportunity to be as loved as Richie did. That is what you two gave him, and he took that with him. You never gave up on him.

Although we don't often understand or see the reasons beyond our immediate experiences, I believe that something greater exists for Richie now... He battled back and forth so many times; his soulful work with you will help reach others who have similar struggles. He would want you to continue to champion the cause and help save the lives of others who are there seeking help, looking for answers, waiting for a sign.

Our paths are a mystery, but I wish Rich Godspeed in this next phase of his journey. You have been a loving mother and did everything that you could to help him lighten the burden of the karma he carried in this life. Now he is released to the Unknowable.

Around the corner there may wait
a new road or a secret gate.

—J.R.R. Tolkien

My Journal (continued)

After all our family and friends started their travels home, after sharing their stories and tears with us, we needed to drive my sister to the airport two hours away. The drive was a blur of rainy hills and words said to soften the hard reality of why she came to visit. Final hugs were received and tears shared as she left to board her plane. On the ride back home, the rain continued but David and I decided to stop at a large farm-type café which boasted stuffed animal heads on the walls, fresh deli' foods, gifts, and canned olives and nuts. We ate a little and wandered the shop to buy green olives.

As we were leaving the gift shop, I opened my umbrella to shield us; then realizing the rain had finally let up for a bit, closed it back down. We synchronously glanced above the rooftops and spied the most colorful and detailed rainbow we had ever seen. Succinctly we whispered, "Richie's come to say he's okay." The rest of the drive home was a dream.

* * *

One of my Blue Jays came to visit today. He perched himself upon a hanging basket dangling next to my bedroom door where I sit on an upper deck to meditate and soak in the late morning sun. The flowers in the hanging planter are dead as the winter night's frost told them they must turn to seed. The Jay hopped right inside the basket picking at twigs and dried leaves until he found just the right mix; then flew away, disappearing into the nearby hedge. I surmised new life would join us soon, emerging from a home being constructed for spring nesting.

The same hedge was the birthplace of twin Jays last spring. We would sit silently still as we watched the mother Jay land on our lower deck to forage until she found just the perfect size of dry dog food bites left from Goldie's bowl, take it gently into her beak and fly into the hedge where her nest of baby Jays awaited. We even spied the two blue fuzzy-down heads bobbing up, displaying wide mouths to receive the unnatural morsels.

I speak to my current Jay each time he lights upon the basket. He cocks his bold head to listen to every word; then pardons himself as he continues his important mission. I thank Mr. Jay for sharing his duties with me. In those few moments, somehow, his life helped to melt the pain of my son's death. This bit of nature's play warmed my heart when it was frozen just minutes before.

How does a parent accept they have outlived their child? One week of grieving, has it been only one week? It seems like a lifetime. As memories pierce my thoughts, it becomes unbearable to comprehend not again will I feel the bear-hugs or see the laughter in Richie's eyes. Sometimes, late at night when the house is silent, I hear a tune singing in my head. It sounds like a Native American song of mourning, although I don't know what that would sound like. With my head slightly raised from the pillow, it sings even more loudly. Rich and I loved all kinds of music; so humming this new tune brings a bit of comfort as I imagine trying to hum it aloud to him. I am sure he and I had several lifetimes together in a Native American Nation.

* * *

"It is through meditation that we may become aware of the existence of the spiritual forces within; that we unlock the door between our physical and spiritual bodies.

Through this door come impulses from the soul, seeking expression in the physical."

—Edgar Cayce

As Cayce states, my life is on a long meditation as I glean from the physical to the spirit around me. The brilliant blossoms on our fruit trees ensure the summer's bounty of nature's desserts. My thoughts go forward for the first time as I remember several friends telling me they would teach me how to can my apricots. This large step into the future without a thought of Richard is welcomed, for I have labored to linger in my mind's past for several weeks. I notice, too, the ground squirrels are awake and dashing in and out of their house-holes in our red rock walls. I am always amazed at how nature renews itself.

David prodded me to ride with him and Goldie to take a long walk through the paths near our home. I accepted begrudgingly. As I became one with the trees and the sky around me, a newfound sense of freedom entered my soul—a freedom releasing the wonderment of life, and of death. Within my metaphysical belief system, there is always a new beginning—call it life, or call it death. As I walk and ponder my beliefs, it becomes clearer than ever just how the completed journey is as important as the beginning one.

* * *

My brain-freeze is beginning to thaw but guilt has pulled up a chair within my heart. Guilt is a strange bedfellow who can make his home quite comfortably in a person's mind and heart. He pokes and prods around dredging up old thoughts and memories of past disappointments and all the old "woulda, coulda, shoulda" routines until there is no room left for truth. Here he sits feeling very proud of himself, thinking his stay will last forever.

In my book *Gifts From the Child Within*, I write about guilt. I explain there are four human emotions which can inhibit, stagnate, stifle, and weaken our progress to heal physically, emotionally, and spiritually. When we allow them power, they hang like dark gray clouds over our existence, shrouding our freedom of choice, hiding our truth, and blocking our Light. These four emotional saboteurs are fear, anger, guilt, and shame. I wrote about how guilt can appear in many different disguises and cause unnecessary pain. I like what one of my favorite authors wrote about guilt. In her book *Guilt is the Teacher, Love is the Lesson* Joan Borysenko shares, "Unhealthy guilt causes life to become organized around the need to avoid fear rather than the desire to share love... In guilt, we say no to life." I understand these wise words, but guilt with all his sabotaging tools has decided to reside within my heart and mind for now bringing with him all his teasing questions of "What if...?"

* * *

One of my dear friends mailed me the perfect book. It is a large book with few pages and filled with lovely homespun pictures of a family going through a loss. There is not a particular type of loss mentioned, which makes the book even more available to those in grieving. The book's title is *Tear Soup: A Recipe for Healing After Loss*. My husband and I both read this delightful story in private as we knew it might touch each of us differently. As I read the pages, many of my own feelings were written in the large text, which I did not expect. I felt that being a counselor for thirty years would assure my grieving the loss of Richard adequately. I was wrong.

Losing a child is not like losing a parent, a friend, or other relative. Losing a child comes with its own set of emotions, none of which seem to fit any of the literature. However, in *Tear Soup*, I was able to feel my pain, touch my grief, and begin to recognize a new found sense of security in my personal spiritual beliefs. Amidst the colorful pictures on tear-proof pages, words of wisdom and insight can be found. Here are a few lines:

> One day as Grandy and Chester were going for a drive, Chester asked, "Mom says you've been making tear soup. What does she mean?"
>
> "Well, tear soup is a way for you to sort through all the different types of feelings and memories you have when you lose someone or something special. Remember when your baby brother died right before he was born and your mom sat for days holding his blanket and weeping? She was making tear soup."
>
> "So what else have you learned by making tear soup, Grandy?"
>
> "I've learned that grief, like a pot of soup, changes the longer it simmers and the more things you put into it... And most importantly, I've learned that there is something down deep within all of us ready to help us survive the things we think we can't survive."

With the help from Grandy, this "old and somewhat wise woman," I am learning to remember my spiritual Self and to reach deep inside for strength.

Friends brought us dinner again tonight; I insisted they stay and eat with us. It felt good to laugh and chat with dear friends again. We talked about their recent travels and memories of Rich, keeping it light and positive. The food was good, the conversation was good, and it felt good to be back in my body once again. The heavy hush of gray cloud-cover finally lifted from my mind.

At midnight, the speckled-star darkness bowed down to a beacon of light as it rose over the hill and through the treetops, landing firm to perch upon her throne to reign the night. I love to follow the phases of the moon. It brings me comfort to know that nature's cycle is still in place. Tomorrow, I will plant some of the many potted plants and flowers delivered to our door by family and friends whose words of solace eased our pain. Planting the ground with all these gifts to honor Richard will add more tears to my soup.

෨෧

"A thing that is universal, that comes to all, cannot be pernicious. To regard death as a disastrous thing would be an indictment of the sanity of nature. Death merely opens the door to a new and wider realm where the evolution of the soul proceeds."

—L. W. Rogers

Most of us have a rather difficult time discussing death, albeit our own or someone we love. My mother studied the spiritual discipline of Theosophy of which I, too, became enchanted. These teachings led me on a lifetime of reading and studying many world religions and metaphysical principles. Due to this background of universal spiritual knowledge, my grieving process of my son's death was painful, but not as difficult as it could have been.

Theosophy teaching states, "As sudden silence gives the consciousness a keener realization of the sound that has just ceased, so death, by its contrast, gives a vivid, realistic touch to life." I know Richard's passing has given me an abundant pause to remember the pleasure we had together. By releasing the difficult times we shared, I can envision him on his new journey, beaming with pride and contentment. Instead of worrying about what could have been, I can sense his presence near me and know his soul has chosen to move forward, beyond our knowing.

* * *

Days seem to run together like stitches on a hem. My backyard Buddhas are smiling in the light spring rain. This rain is not like the dark hard droplets of winter's deluge but a baby rain silently falling from beneath white clouds. Somehow, nature has given me a respite, a time to cleanse inside and out—I am grateful. As I listen to the enlightened chimes of bamboo hanging near our bedroom deck, Mr. Jay appears. He fluffs his blue coat to shield himself and talks to me of the new eggs in the hedge, then departs to find his favorite black seeds in the feeder.

If there ever is a conclusion to the pending "unified field theory" being examined by world physicists, I hope they include the cycle of life, death, and rebirth within their equations regarding nature, human or otherwise. To me, all humankind is shaped by this simple truth. In physics, a *field* refers to an area under the influence of some *force*—rain, electricity, astronomy. Many have tried to combine all known phenomena to explain nature and its behavior as a single unified field theory to create a comprehensive view of how our universe runs. I think all of nature—life, death, and rebirth included—is a product of free will.

For those of us who believe that each soul is created by a Divine Force, the above thought is a given. For those of us who believe there is free will provided by this Divine Source, there already is a unified field theory. After reading the enlightening little book *The Shack* by William P. Young, my mind cannot be more positive that we live in a universal pool of free will. Each soul is a separate entity unto itself to choose how to react to each event which crosses its path. Each soul as a separate entity creates its life as it feels guided, remembering its Creator always forgives the choices which *seem* to hinder ultimate growth.

As Young's God in *The Shack* comments,

> "A created being can only take what already exists and from it fashion something different... there are millions of reasons to allow pain and hurt and suffering rather than to eradicate them, but most of those reasons can only be understood within each person's story... I will use every choice you make for the ultimate good and the most loving outcome."

I do not profess to know the ultimate theories of nature, human or otherwise; but, I do know my son chose, on some spiritual level, to leave his struggling life to find peace in another phase of his soul's journey. He left behind his alcoholism, his pain, and his loved-ones, knowing he would meet with us again, perhaps in another lifetime, perhaps in the clouds of heaven. I know wherever we meet, we will recognize each other and be bonded by this lifetime as mother and son.

"You would know the secret of death. But how shall you find it unless you seek it in the heart of life?

The owl whose night-bound eyes are blind unto the day cannot unveil the mystery of light.

If you would indeed behold the spirit of death, open your heart wide unto the body of life.

For life and death are one, even as the river and the sea are one."

—Kahlil Gibran

My Journal (continued)

Our fruit trees kept their promise of serving up summer's desserts. As I sit on the deck in awe of the evening sunset, remembering my pain from only six months prior, a tune visits my heart and I think of Richard. He has entered the realm of the unknowable, yet he sits beside me, listening to my attempt to hum the notes he has sent me. Remember the song which came to my lips the day after he died, which I felt was a Native American ritual song? I discovered through my friend, Sage Runningbear, who is a Pomo Native American shaman, that it was indeed an old Lakota mourning song. What a gift my son gave to me; that tune drifted through my mind for months inculcating my emotional flow. Rich makes himself known to us in many ways—a faint smell of cologne, a song on the radio, a meaningful dream, and Goldie's silent stare into nothingness only she can see.

Another song which enters my mind repeatedly is Groban's "February Song." Rich slipped from our reality in February, and these lyrics, as well as the music, touch my heartstrings:

> Where has that old friend gone?
> Tell him it won't be long 'til he opens his eyes
> I never want to let you down
> Forgive me if I slip away
> I promise I'll come back to you one day.

* * *

I glance out the window and spy a squirrel on the lower deck, scurrying with a white sock in its mouth. I must remember not to leave our dirty shoes and socks outside. Our animal friends are much too friendly sometimes and take advantage of our neighborly ways.

We have a fountain on the deck that plays its continual water song as it splashes onto the smooth flat round rocks. My mind gets lost in the unending pools of circling liquid; then awakens to take note to clean the bird feathers from the edges to ensure the next visit looks inviting.

Rich's birthday passed (May 7th). Again he appeared in our reality by ringing our bedroom telephone *once* to awaken us at exactly to the minute when I gave birth to him forty-one years ago, 5:20am. Just as the rainbow arrived so vividly on our trip home from the airport, he comes now and then to pronounce his presence in mystical ways he knows we will recognize. He is always with us. Twenty years ago, when he turned twenty-one, I gave him a crystal on a chain which he wore around his neck. I found it within his belongings the other day. The crystal pendant had a tiny flat gold ornament attached to it with an "R" etched in black. A few days ago, I placed the ornament on my chain next to the gold *OM* tear drop. I touch it often.

I no longer entertain the saboteur of guilt; I no longer cry at the thought of the smile which danced across his face, or the sound of a song while driving in the car. The cooking pot for my tear soup has long been put away in the cupboard. There are still clothes and belongings to sort through but there is no rush. Rich's friends call occasionally to ask if we need help with anything and share with us how they miss their friend. But, thankfully, there are new fawns chasing butterflies on the hill, baby quail dashing behind grownups, and Mr. Jay who tends to his new brood to keep us company. Soon, he will need to let his fledglings fly their own journey, as Richard's has just begun.

Finishing my Journal, I find the summer's lake is bath-warm enticing me to float and stay until the sun says goodnight. Summer has touched the lake's dress, spilling colors of blue and mint green while lifting its skirt to reveal white foam ruffles. Ducks bounce to the water's rhythm; then strut to shore to bask in the heat of the sun. Hot air balloons paint the sky with reds, yellows, and purples floating over the lake, hanging like an angel's amulet reflecting on the water below. Lying in the shade of a tree, a rainbow sail floats across the sky. I widen my view to realize it is a reflection and glance to spy a wind-surfer's rig. This reminds me of the rainbow Rich sent us just six months earlier.

I also reflect on the pages in this book and pray they are of use to at least as many readers as the writers who submitted their soul stories. I reflect on the seasons which have passed and of nature's cyclic harmony presenting me with ways to ease my suffering. *Nature*, with all her truth and reliability, has been that *Something More* for me. I am blessed and honored with her visits. I reflect on how she has joined me along my path, presenting me with the gentleness of deer, curiosity and persistence of the squirrel, the food gifts of her bounty, Mr. Jay's compassion, a meaningful message in a drop of rain, and the acceptance surrounding a new beginning, even in death.

ॐ✥

"May my suffering substitute for all similar types of suffering that sentient beings may have to undergo.

May I, by experiencing this, be able to save all other sentient beings from having to undergo the same suffering."

—His Holiness The Dalai Lama

As the Dalai Lama states so eloquently, I too hope that our suffering might help others lessen theirs. If all those who have managed to rid themselves of an addiction were to help only one other child, teen, or adult to face the reality of being addicted to a drug and/or alcohol and guide him or her toward recovery, our addiction population would diminish substantially. If you are addicted to a substance and wish to obtain help, please allow yourself to ask for it—help is all around you.

Living with an addiction is a spiritual journey. As stated earlier, I believe no one takes that first pill, drink, snort, inhale, or injection, thinking they will become addicted. Perhaps a trauma or pain in their life, which was not addressed or healed, guided them to their self-destructive behavior. How should we view a person with an addiction? As a low-life or as someone who is less than ourselves? That *choice* is yours. I choose to view those with an addiction as *missing their mark*. They have wandered off their original path onto a side-street called *self-hatred*. I believe it is our responsibility to help them envision a new pathway, a new direction filled with self-esteem, self-worth, and self-love.

The following parable by Portia Nelson can help us all check our own life-saboteurs, it is called "Autobiography in Five Short Chapters." (see next page)

Chapter 1

I walk down the street. There is a deep hole in the sidewalk and I fall in. I am lost. I am helpless. It is not my fault. It takes me forever to find a way out.

Chapter 2

I walk down the same street. There is a deep hole in the sidewalk. I pretend I do not see it. I fall in again. I cannot believe I am in the same place, but it is not my fault. It still takes me a long time to get out.

Chapter 3

I walk down the same street. There is a deep hole in the sidewalk. I see it. I still fall in. It is a habit, but my eyes are open and I know where I am. It is my fault. I get out quickly.

Chapter 4

I walk down the same street. There is a deep hole in the sidewalk. I walk around it.

Chapter 5

I walk down a different street.

What can *you* do to help those addicted to drugs or alcohol? Guide and direct them toward a different street.

11 Living the Moment, Seeking the Truth

"I always believe that each individual human being has some kind of responsibility for humanity as a whole... Through my own profession, I try my best to contribute as much as I can. This proceeds without my being concerned whether another person agrees with my philosophy or not.

Some people may be very much against my belief, my philosophy, but I feel all right. So long as I see that a human being suffers or has needs, I shall contribute as much as I can to contribute to their benefit."

—His Holiness The Dalai Lama

There is a little book titled *The Knight in Rusty Armor* that I have given to dozens of my patients through the years, which contains an insightful fairy tale. It goes something like this:

Once upon a time long ago, there lived a Knight. He was a very good Knight, slaying all the dragons and rescuing many damsels in distress. He fought with bravery for many decades, wearing his trusty metal armor. The Knight fought hard throughout the land and all the while his suit of armor was taken off less and less. Soon, he became so used to his armor he never took it off, even when sleeping! Eventually, he even had to be fed through the visor of the helmet because he did not want to remove it. The Knight became so distracted with his job of fighting demons and dragons, that he soon distanced himself entirely from his family and friends.

One day, the Knight's armor became immovable and no one could get close to him. He only recognized and acknowledged his own life, that of fighting dragons to receive praise across the land. Finally, there came a day when the Knight desired to set his armor aside to enjoy the freedom he remembered from earlier days, but the armor had rusted and it could not be removed! He tried everything to rid himself of his heavy burden but it was no use, he was stuck with the cold, ridged armor.

Then one day, the Knight was told of a magician who might help him. He made the long treacherous journey to the land where a man named Merlin could be found. When they met, Merlin told the Knight, "You are so afraid... that is why you put on the armor in the first place." The Knight in his rusty armor was instructed to take a new path—the path of Truth. This path contained many castles to explore such as the castle of Silence, Knowledge, and Will & Daring. Within these castles, the Knight was dared to fight dragons of Fear and Doubt and meet several unknown beings that would help him release his own internal demons which would help shed his body, mind, and soul of the rusty armor.

Happily, our courageous Knight was able to find and conquer all the castles, slay all the demons, and confront his own fears. Soon, his armor began to fall to the ground, piece by piece, until he was set completely free. "For the first time, he saw his life clearly, without judgment and without excuses... he accepted full responsibility for his life, for the influence that people had had on it, and for the events that had shaped it." The Knight learned he could no longer blame his mistakes and misfortunes on anyone or anything outside himself. The recognition that he was the cause, not the effect, gave him a new feeling of power. He was now unafraid. The Knight returned to his family a peaceful and happy man.

This is a good story to which we all can relate. Whether addicted to drugs, alcohol, food, sex, gambling, or any other substance or behavior, we can allow ourselves to choose a different direction, a new path to set us free of our demons. Our choices are like specific degrees on our life compass of *causes* taking us on journeys yet envisioned. Our test then, is to learn how to choose the paths which result in a long positive journey, or *effect*. How can we do this? We do this by using all our senses and available support before making decisions. We must investigate the possible outcomes; envision the results; seek knowledge from others; and, go within to trust our intuition.

Just as the Knight with his rusty armor learned he was controlling his life—good and bad—we can choose to wake-up and recognize that we are co-creating our reality through our actions and reactions. Every choice we make, every path we take is paving the way for our future journeys—good and bad. The Knight learned that he was hiding from his fears by putting on a mask and armor to distance himself from the ones he loved, and from himself. He found by exploring new lands and new paths, albeit a difficult journey, that he could make more positive choices for himself. He took his power back and released his old beliefs and patterns, freeing himself from his enslavement.

Living with a drug or alcohol addiction is one of the most difficult choices a person can make. Those who have done so have a spiritual path which claims much hardship and suffering. Gary Zukav wrote, "As you face your deepest struggles, you reach for your highest goal." This is true for any who choose to recognize their own fears and to accept their own truth. This is also true of those addicts desperately shouting for help but their screams going unheard. Facing our deepest fears, doubts, and struggles is the soul-work of each life; to an addict, it is never-ending.

Zukav continues his wise words instructing how those with an addiction can free themselves, "This is the way out of an addiction: Walk yourself through your reality step by step. Make yourself aware of the consequences of your decisions, and choose accordingly." *Looking forward always brings us to our karmic future.*

Attaining emotional freedom is not an easy task. For most of us, this sense of peace arrives only after much inner work. While in my fifties, it became clear to me that I could no longer allow my emotions to have unfettered freedom over my life. Between the loss of my mother and an ensuing lawsuit, battling a physical illness, and struggling with my son's addiction, I knew I needed to sway my emotional state-of-being away from Fear and back to Trust. I enlisted many of the holistic tools and techniques mentioned in this book, and others, to help guide me back to my peaceful center. I recognized I needed to free myself from the demons and dragons of Doubt and Fear.

Psychiatrist and author Judith Orloff explains in her book *Emotional Freedom* that emotional freedom is the act of, "...increasing your ability to love by cultivating positive emotions and being able to compassionately witness and transform negative ones, whether they're yours or another's." And, that with true emotional freedom, "...you can *choose* to react constructively rather than relinquishing your command of the situation whenever your buttons get pushed, as most people do." I am still learning to do this.

One of my favorite poets, Patrick Lane, bravely narrates his first book *What the Stones Remember: A Life Rediscovered*. In it, Lane describes his journey of twelve months while attempting sobriety for the first time in his life; he was in his sixties at the time. His bravery at attempting to attain physical, spiritual, and emotional freedom is heartfelt. His prose reads like poetry as he pens words which dance a desperate rhythm in the reader's mind. He shows us his exhausting pain at choosing to abstain from his favorite drink, vodka. Lane's choices were not easy that year; they did not just appear before him each morning as sunshine on the window pane. He had to consciously choose *not* to taste the sweet liquid he had forbidden himself. Going sober was the hardest choice of Lane's life.

Here are a few lines from Lane's valiant struggle which I so honor:

The power the body has to go willingly toward pain is something no one understands, not even the addict himself.

Without the past I can't learn to live in the unfolding present... The clear moments of memory must be understood. It is only then they can be let go.

...depression still creeps like a mouse under my skin.

My self was gone, only my spirit remained to watch its body trying to die.

My addiction sleeps with its claws in my mind.

"Using the breath to bring us back to the present moment takes no time at all, only a shift in attention. But great adventures await you if you give yourself a little time to string moments together, breath by breath, moment to moment."
—Jon Kabat-Zinn

I am a firm believer of modern holistic health practices. I often refer patients to colleagues dealing in the holistic field to ensure a full range of healing and recovery experiences. I guide them to find their own answers and choices by dealing with issues and decisions on all levels—body, mind, spirit, and emotions. I suggest and refer them to seek physical exams; explore massage and acupuncture; discover biofeedback; experience Reiki, art therapy, hypnotherapy, spiritual ritual, positive affirmations, and other methods of holistic integration. I introduce them to yoga, numerology, astrology, divination tools, dreamwork, and meditation, if they are interested in new ways to explore their spiritual and emotional self, and are willing to find new directions toward their recovery.

This holistic methodology can be offered to all those addicted to drugs and alcohol, perhaps directing them in their choice to become free of their addiction. Currently, I am aware of only a few models of holistic addiction treatment centers but would like to see more in the future. I work with clients of one such center. This center offers their residents holistic methods including raw food nutrition, massage and meditation, yoga and martial arts, live blood analysis, and spiritual counseling. I enjoy visiting the center to instruct and guide those who seek inner-work such as regression therapy, inner child emotional release therapy, chakra balancing, dreamwork, divination, and ritual experiences and tools.

My dear friend and coauthor of *Addiction: What's Really Going On?* Deborah McCloskey was a drug and alcohol counselor. She felt that using all avenues to help those addicted is both compassionate and necessary to ensure all levels of support. She would go to great lengths to help her clients make constructive choices and offer new directions for them to discover.

One story in the book is about how she was able to surmise that some women who were claiming to need a higher dose of methadone because of various monthly symptoms were, in fact, experiencing menopause. She would also tell clients about certain herbal remedies to use while detoxing and relayed many other ways to counter her clients' fears, doubts, and insecurities which seemed to appear like fire-breathing dragons from their tormented consciousness. She offered them balanced, holistic avenues toward their sobriety, herself becoming a Merlin-of-sorts and the "counselor to get" at the clinic.

These methods are not difficult to offer or master; sometimes a simple solution is the best. Deborah suggested to one lonely older gentleman that he might like to take the bus to a different town each week and experience new adventures. This simple suggestion afforded the man a new outlook of hope to his otherwise dull existence. To another addict trying to obtain sobriety, she offered a tablet of paper and colored pens to draw his emotions and fears so he might learn how to let them go. All of these holistic, as well as, traditional counseling tools therapists have on their palettes could be shared with our addicted population to help them paint their futures bright with sobriety.

As you have read throughout the stories within this book, many of those addicted to drugs and alcohol found their own path to walk with sobriety. Some chose to walk with that Something More; some with 12-Step groups; some chose better diets and exercise; while others learned to cope with the stumbles of relapse through regimens of detoxification. All will not choose the same path; but all paths taken can lead to a life without addiction. *If a different path than the current is not chosen, sobriety cannot be found.*

"And while I stood there, I saw more than I can tell and I understood more than I saw; for I was seeing in a sacred manner the shapes of all things in the spirit, and the shape of all shapes as they must live together like one being."

—Black Elk

I believe we can become acquainted with new ideas, new pathways toward recovery, by using different levels of exposure to the human healing experience. John Dupuy, a pioneer in the field of holistic or integral healing has developed an addiction recovery model he terms Integral Recovery. Dupuy states with this new recovery treatment model, "...we can be sure we aren't neglecting anything that might later sabotage our efforts" toward a complete and long-lasting recovery. In this process of Integral Recovery based on philosopher Ken Wilber's Integral Vision theory, each patient explores four quadrants or areas which are used as a diagnostic tool.

The first area looks at any damage or harm to the brain and physical body of the addict and introduces therapeutic restorative measures to help heal and balance the damage done by the disease. This includes exercise, nutritional supplements, a healthy diet, yoga, bodywork, and enhanced meditation. The second area addresses the issues of mental chaos, anger, anxiety, depression, hatred of others, and hatred of self. These internal experiences need to be explored, both as symptoms and causative factors through such practices as individual therapy, group therapy, meditation, shadow work, trauma work, and cognitive learning about the disease of addiction itself. The third area covers the usual devastation in the patient's relationships due to the negative behaviors caused by the progression of the disease. Here the introduction to family therapy, couples therapy, and amends-making is needed to restore the shredded social fabric. Lastly, there are often legal, financial, and other systems-related problems that must be addressed. Dupuy states:

All four quadrants have to be dealt with as part of an overall Integral Treatment program. Again, since the disease affects all four areas, any treatment program that does not effectively address the integral whole will be partial and ultimately ineffective. By healing and balancing the four quadrants of their lives and working the four essential lines—body, mind, heart, and soul—in a life-long Integral Recovery Practice, patients can begin their healing and transformation.

Somewhere in this process of transcending within the goal of Integral Recovery, the individual transforms beyond simple sobriety into a quest to become one's best and truest self. The goal of practice is no longer mere survival and stopping the progression of the disease, but self-actualization in the relative world and Self-realization in the timeless present.

Dupuy adds that in our nation alone, two hundred billion dollars is spent on addiction recovery each year. Just imagine where that money could be spent if our nation's addiction problem was eradicated. I can imagine hungry children being fed; schools properly maintained and furnished; health care available for all citizens; senior care facilities with up-to-date medical equipment; and colleges available for all youth.

Holistic or alternative medicine is becoming a more common theme in health care today. Many use the term Alternative Medicine or Integral Health to define this shift toward a more balanced avenue to wholeness. Author of *Integral Health: The Path to Human Flourishing* Dr. Elliott Dacher states, "To transform health and life, we must shift our gaze inward, where we will find the ever-present source of exceptional health and healing." Dacher addresses the possibility of our striving for authentic happiness and a genuine wholeness for everyone. He continues, "We are standing empty-handed in the midst of great wealth, satisfied with a sliver of what is possible, thinking it's all there is, all that is possible. We are of the extraordinary, and yet each day, we settle for the ordinary."

Dacher's reference to an *inward gaze* stems from our ability to shift our awareness from an outside view to our inner authentic self. What is our authentic self? I would like to think this refers to one's true Self that is within each of us from birth to death. This is the Self we sometimes hide so others won't see our weakness or fears; it is the Self we show only to a select few who have gained our trust. The authentic self is who we strive to become, all the while knowing it is who we already are. It is that aspect of our Self discovered when we look inward in silence. Can an addict transcend his addiction to reach for his authentic self, to become all he can be? I would not have attempted to write this book if I felt otherwise.

"True world peace can only be achieved through peace of mind. And peace of mind springs from a genuine realization that all human beings are brothers and sisters.

Different ideologies and different political or economic systems are only secondary; the most important point is that we are all the same human beings, living on one small planet."

—His Holiness The Dalai Lama

As the quote above states, everyone on this planet has a connection to one another. And, as the planet becomes smaller and smaller through technology, our means of helping others become larger and easier. Our spiritual connection, no matter what religion, or no religion, is evident throughout the world. Consider humanity's undying devotion to music and the arts; consider humanity's strength against hunger and starvation or its fight against AIDs, child abuse, or terrorism. The fact that there is a spiritual connection between human beings is not questioned, but questions regarding drug and alcohol addiction remain:

- How can we help our addicted population?

- Why do our children decide to choose their first snort, drink, injection, or smoke?

- Who whispered in society's ear that addicts need to stay addicted to their drug of choice in order to maintain a level of power over the populous?

- Who among us can say they did not, at one moment in time, need the help and compassion of another?

Allow me to address these questions with more questions:

- If we do *not* find the means to help our addicted population, will the numbers of addicts escalate to reach a majority of our planet's population?

- Why can't we ask our addicted population to assist in reaching our younger generations, warning them against taking that first snort, drink, injection, or smoke?

- Will governments ever hear our cries for crackdowns on drug lords and street corner trafficking, or will they continue to feed *their* addiction to greed?

- What can *you* do to help those addicted?

If you can relate to just one story in this book, you have experienced compassion, either *from* another or *for* another. Now, what can you do to help your neighbor addicted to alcohol? What can you do to help the kid down the block that is tempted to try pot for the first time? How can you help the lonely guy sitting on the shelter steps trying desperately to stop his cocaine habit?

Compassion is not a foreign expression; it is not sitting on a shelf, waiting for you to unwrap its kindness. Compassion is part of your authentic self. It resides in the heart and likes to be introduced to others frequently. His Holiness The Dalai Lama professes that deep compassion is the true path to happiness and enlightenment. He states:

> "Once one has become profoundly moved by great compassion and loving-kindness, and had one's heart stirred by altruistic thoughts, one must pledge to devote oneself to freeing all beings from the suffering they endure..."

There is no such thing as a problem without a gift for you
in its hands. You seek problems because you need their gifts.
—Richard Bach

I read in an article that scientific research is testing the ability of using our own body cells to repair damaged organs and parts of our body. And, that stem cell research is validating the reality of cell consciousness. In 1985, Robert Becker, a pioneer in the field of bioelectric science introduced *The Body Electric*. In this book, Becker spoke about the use of electrical impulses stimulating cell re-growth. With each new decade, more scientific research is validating our understanding of the body-mind connection. How can we use this vast range of knowledge to help those addicted? One day, will we be able to change the cells in the brain of those addicted to drugs or alcohol to alleviate the desire for their substance?

Recently, research studies uncovered an alcohol trigger site in the brain that researchers have known about but the exact location and visualization was unknown until now. Scientists at the Salk Institute for Biological Studies have uncovered that alcohol directly interacts with a specific nook inside an ion channel protein, which plays a significant role in brain functions that are related to drug abuse and seizures. The study's lead researcher, Paul A. Slesinger, Ph.D., is an associate professor in the Peptide Biology Laboratory at the Salk Institute. He explains that the discovery of this structure "...could lead researchers to develop new therapeutic treatments for alcoholism, drug addiction, and epilepsy." Perhaps, with new findings like these, our world can be free from drug and alcohol addiction. I would like to think this is a possibility.

Researching our senior population, we find many of our older generation addicted to the false reality of legal prescriptions and/or alcohol's buzz. We certainly need a breakthrough in research soon. More than six million individuals over the age of sixty-five are addicted to alcohol in our nation. This figure will increase dramatically as the "baby-boomers" approach their older years. Are we ready for this increase?

Also, many of our younger children are daring each other to "Just try it; it's fun." Our older teens are using marijuana and alcohol with an increase in the use of prescription drugs. The average age for first experimentation with drugs is thirteen years. We need to target this group of pre-addicted youth through all social media, as well as, within the family unit. They find their substances through the

Internet, on the corner, in the park, at local pain clinics, on school grounds, and in your medicine cabinets. This age group has discovered that the use of computers allows them to talk to virtual strangers, which gives them a feeling of inhibition unknown to older generations. They can disclose secrets, pictures, and even deal drugs easily every day without a smudge of guilt because of their anonymity.

As sad as it is, I hope the drug-related deaths of celebrities such as Michael Jackson, Elvis Presley, Heath Ledger, Jimi Hendrix, Anna Nicole Smith, Janis Joplin, and so many others will someday make an impact on our younger population regarding drug and alcohol addiction. Stories from unknown people like those in this book are no different than the celebrities above. Their lives, and ours, will continue to impact one another all over the world.

What remains important is to live your life in the present moment, truthfully, and choose to consciously create your reality with peace and compassion. Spiritual teacher Thich Nhat Hanh put it this way:

"Many of us think that happiness is not possible in the present moment. Most of us believe that there are a few more conditions that need to be met before we can be happy. This is why we are sucked into the future and are not capable of being present in the here and now. This is why we step over many of the wonders of life. If we keep running away into the future, we cannot be in touch with the many wonders of life—we cannot be in the present moment where there is healing, transformation, and joy."

Epilogue

There are a few noteworthy topics I would like to address in the aftermath of this book's completion. It has been noted that an increase in the numbers of those addicted to drugs, especially opiate dependence, are expected to rise significantly in the next few years due to our nation's soldiers returning from duty in Iraq and Afghanistan. This is because Afghanistan produces approximately ninety-two percent of the world's heroin supply; so sadly, we can expect many of our veterans to return home with an opioid addiction. Are we prepared for this influx? Statistics and research say we are not.

Recent research released by the National Center on Addiction and Substance Abuse (CASA) at Columbia University states that the vast majority of the estimated 467 billion dollars in substance-abuse related spending by our government was spent on the *consequences* of alcohol, tobacco, and other drug use, *not* on their treatment and prevention. Those consequences include homeless shelters, emergency room treatment, hospital bed occupancy, incarcerations, court and legal issues, social services and family welfare. This statistic is mind-boggling, considering our drastic need for more preventative measures directed toward our younger generations and the overflowing population of our substance abuse county-aid financed treatment programs. There is an abundant number of private facilities which are readily available for those who can pay either out-of-pocket or have medical insurance which will cover costly addiction related treatment, but not enough low cost or government-assisted treatment programs, which is what our veterans will need.

The public can become a part of our nation's fight against drug and alcohol addiction by writing to their government representatives, local newspapers, and state and county-aid programs to voice their opinions and concerns. The billions of dollars stated above are available and should be used to support existing substance abuse programs and to start new ones in local communities which are low or no cost to those in need. It is time for those who have been affected by drug and alcohol addiction in some manner, to step up and make sure every child has an updated and realistic education surrounding the use of drugs and alcohol. It is time for us to use our influence and our compassion to make sure each individual (veteran or not) addicted to drugs or alcohol who desires to enter a treatment program can, in fact, easily locate a reputable facility in his or her local community. I stress the word *reputable* because of a recent discovery uncovering documentation surrounding a prison/drug treatment and research facility which used questionable procedures in the past.

In 2008, a review and somewhat of a scandal was released surrounding a prison in Kentucky which was in operation from 1935 to 1975 that was a home for thousands of addicts and alcoholics. It was called "The Narcotic Farm." Film footage, photo slides, literature, and other information was found depicting halls of horror showing men hooked to electrical-shock machines and given drugs such as LSD to discover the "cure" for drug and alcohol addiction. The experimentation on humans was (and most probably is) unprecedented with the testing of the effects and addiction potential of most all known drugs. Over four decades, convicted drug addicts (two-thirds convicts) and patient volunteers endured experimentation involving heroin, morphine, cocaine, alcohol, barbiturates, marijuana, sleeping pills, tranquilizers, and LSD. The facility's closure coincided with the Congressional investigation into LSD research.

No doubt many positive benefits were reaped from the Narcotic Farm such as learning about the body, mind, and emotional response to certain drugs and stimulants; connecting others with addictions to abate feelings of isolation, and the education, work ethic, and sharing between those with a similar mindset. However, the thought of my loved one going into a facility such as the Narcotic Farm is not as positive. I would like to see facilities with much more compassion, freedom, respect, and education offered to our addicted population. Also, as mentioned, the use of alternative and holistic methods could be offered a client in an out-patient program or a patient in residence. Reading or listening only to *one* addiction story is enough to realize that our nation is long overdue in manifesting adequate and *financially available* treatment programs for our addiction population.

I also wish to address the issue of planned interventions. Many argue against the process of forming a cadre of loved ones and professionals to convince the person addicted to drugs or alcohol that they can "beat" their dependency. This group argues that only the addict himself can choose to take that jump toward sobriety. They are right. However, if we ignore our loved one's addiction, or even encourage it with co-dependent or enabling behavior, isn't that just giving them permission to continue their addiction?

To be clear, I am in favor of the intervention process allowing loved ones to voice their personal issues surrounding the addictive behavior and how it affects their lives. We watch in awe as the professional interventionists on the popular television program *Intervention 911* work their magic amid the tears, screams, and prayers to elicit acknowledgement from the addict that supervised treatment may be needed. Perhaps, this type of intervention can urge addicted individuals to discover how they are impacting other's lives, not just their own. This discovery might be the turning point needed to guide the addicted individual toward that first step on the recovery path, if he indeed chooses to walk it.

Sadly, we cannot forget the celebrities like Michael Jackson, Heath Ledger, Elvis Presley, Anna Nicole Smith, and so many others, who have died due to their addictions before loved ones, or medical professionals, realized the extent of their addiction to drugs and/or alcohol. Those are only the names we recognize—there are thousands of others who die under these same circumstances. If the loved ones of those with a drug or alcohol addiction "out" their family members or friends—either individually or with the aid of an intervention group—perhaps some deaths could be prevented. This may be the right time for you to urge your loved one to come out-of-the-closet with their addiction and seek help.

Another topic to explore is how we deal with our addicted population which has committed criminal acts. Our jails and prisons are overflowing with men and women who have been, and are, heavily addicted to drugs. Currently, there are 7.1 million adults in prison or on probation and about 1.2 million of them are nonviolent drug abusers. Only approximately twenty percent of those in prison receive treatment for their addiction. Many of them are incarcerated for years only to be released to begin their cycle of addiction and criminal behavior anew.

Recent studies reviewed by the National Institute on Drug Abuse

(NIDA) found heroin addicts treated with methadone while in a treatment program in prison continued their treatment when they were released. Also, that addicts who received no treatment were seven times more likely than those who received treatment to become addicted to heroin again once back on the streets, and three times more likely to commit a crime and land back in prison.

The Drug Court model is becoming more visible to the public as an alternative for those addicted individuals who have broken the law. In lieu of a traditional justice court system, where the majority of those found guilty are sent to prison, the Drug Court system actually keeps the individual in a rehabilitation facility for a length of time to assure their sobriety for up to one year. The individuals are treated as human beings, not low-lifes and thrown in a jail cell. There are required court appearances, random drug testing, therapy for family members, supervision by those familiar with addiction procedures, and help in getting and staying straight and sober. The rewards are immeasurable when seen though the eyes of an addict becoming sober for perhaps the first time in his or her life. The Drug Court literature states:

> Although eligibility guidelines vary, most Drug Courts do not consider violent offenders. Adult criminal Drug Courts usually consider both drug and drug-driven offenses. And where offenses involve victims, the consent of the victim and payment of restitution is typically mandatory. Drug Courts are the most effective justice intervention in treating drug-addicted people. Drug Courts reduce drug use. Drug Courts reduce crime. Drug Courts save money. Drug Courts restore lives. Drug Courts save children and reunite families. Drug Courts serve a fraction of the estimated 1.2 million drug-addicted people currently involved in the justice system. To truly break the cycle of drugs and crime in America, we must put a Drug Court within reach of every American in need. (NADCP)

If you wish to find more information or a specific court's eligibility guidelines, see the National Association of Drug Courts (NADCP) listed in the Resources. Also, visit the web site for "All Rise" which describes how instead of imprisoning an addict, Drug Courts insert hope and support into the very lives of people who the traditional justice system says are hopeless.

Finally, I want to share the latest findings relating addiction treatment and its costs within our health care system. I am sure many reading my plea for more available addiction treatment in our nation would disagree, stating our health care programs cannot afford more policy changes. I would like to address this issue with the findings from the Open Society Institute (July 2009), which is designed to create an awareness of—and increase resources to close—the treatment gap found in the addiction recovery field.

Closing the Addiction Treatment Gap (CATG) is a national program working with nine other organizations to expand addiction treatment for those who desire to reach out for help. Currently, four out of five Americans who need drug and alcohol addiction treatment are unable to get it. The CATG initiative aims to mobilize public support for expanded treatment by increasing public funding, broadening insurance coverage, and achieving greater program efficiency.

Looking at the findings of recent literature from the CATG, we find "Effective addiction treatment can contribute to improving quality and containing costs in reforming America's health care system." The research found the following health care justifications and cost-effective benefits when addiction treatment ensues:

- Reduced emergency room care costs. Almost two million ER visits a year are associated with drug abuse.

- Reduced hospital stays. One out of every fourteen hospital stays are related to substance abuse.

- If addictions are untreated, the person's medical care becomes fragmented, inefficient, and results in health risks which are much more costly in the long run.

- Treating addictions will save money from the reduced costs of treating other general medical and chronic illness conditions.

- Reduced total medical costs. The Kaiser Permanente study found addiction treatment reduced total medical costs twenty-six percent, billions of dollars.

These findings support my efforts in challenging Americans to stand up and be counted: Ask for help if needed, seek help for loved ones, and voice your opinions regarding addiction treatment availability and affordability. If we recognize addiction to drugs and alcohol as a treatable condition, we must also accept the responsibility for that treatment. By treating our addiction population within a more available and cost-effective manner in the future, we will garnish both better overall health outcomes and significantly reduce the growing number of individuals struggling with a drug or alcohol addiction.

There is No Shame, No Blame, in a death from an addiction--Just Love. At the one year anniversary of Rich's death, February 23rd, 2010, I wrote this poem:

For Rich

It has been a year since your face wore its infectious smile
It has been a year since your arms have wrapped around my waist
I have grieved; I have cried; I have watched time go by
Hoping you send me another message from above.

I know your spirit is exploring new vistas
But mine is still heavy with remembrances
I hear a song we shared and my heart leaps
I say your name aloud, the air holds it tight.

It has been a year since we prayed for your happiness
It has been a year since we bid you good night
Dear son please know your life is honored
We will meet you soon in flight.

Bibliography

Alcoholics Anonymous World Services. *Alcoholic anonymous: the big book*. New York: Alcoholics Anonymous World Services, Inc., 1976.

Anderson, U. S. *Three magic words*. Hollywood: Melvin Powers Wilshire Book Company, 1954.

Ashley, Nancy. *A seth workbook: create your own reality*. New York: Prentice Hall Press, 1987.

Bach, Richard. *Illusions: the adventures of a reluctant messiah*. New York: Dell Publishing Company, Inc., 1979.

Bach, Richard. *Messiah's handbook: reminders for the advanced soul*. Charlottesville: Hampton Roads Publishing Company, Inc., 2004.

Becker, Robert O. and Gary Selden. *The body electric: electromagnetism and the foundation of life*. New York: William Morrow & Company, Inc., 1985.

Blum, Ralph H. *The book of runes*. New York: St. Martin's Press, 1993.

Borysenko, Joan. *Guilt is the teacher, love is the lesson*. New York: Warner Books Inc., 1990.

Burroughs, Augusten. *Dry*. New York: St. Martin's Press, 2003.

"Clarity" Magazine. Sacramento: Ananda Sangha Church of Self-Realization, 2008.

Combs, Jared. *Incomprehensible demoralization: an addict pharmacist's journey to recovery*. Bloomington: Xlibris Book Publishing, 2008.

Dacher, Elliot S. *Integral health: the path to human flourishing*. Laguna Beach: Basic Health Publications, Inc., 2006.

DeLorey, Christine. *Life cycles: your emotional journey to freedom and happiness*. Randolph: Osmos Books, 2000.

DeWitt, Gail M. *Where spirituality & recovery meet*. Montgomery: E-Book Time, 2007.

Dyer, Wayne W. *The power of intention: learning to co-create your world your way*. Carlsbad: Hay House, Inc., 2004.

Ellis, Albert and Emmett Velten. *Rational steps to quitting alcohol*. Fort Lee: Barricade Books, Inc., 1992.

Emerson, Sue, Editor. "Addiction Treatment Forum." Mundelein: Clinco Communications, Inc., Vol. 18, #1, 2009.

Ferguson, Marilyn, Contributor. Russell E. DiCarlo, Editor. *Towards a new world view*. Las Vegas: Epic Publishing Company, Inc., 1996.

Fisher, Robert. *The knight in rusty armor*. Hollywood: Melvin Powers Wilshire Book Publishing, 1990.

Ford, Debbie. *The dark side of the light chasers: reclaiming your power, creativity, brilliance, and dreams*. New York: Riverhead Books, 1998.

Genetic Science Learning Center. *Learn Genetics™* "The Mouse Party" An interactive video on drug analysis. University of Utah, 2006.

Gibran, Kahlil. *The prophet*. New York: Quality Paperback Book Club, 1955/original printing 1923.

Groban, Josh. "Awake" album. Social Development Music, 2006.

H. H. the Dalai Lama. *An open heart: practicing compassion in everyday life*. New York: Time Warner Trade Publishing, 2001.

H. H. the Dalai Lama and Howard C. Cutler. *The art of happiness: a handbook for living*. New York: Riverhead Books/Penguin Putnam, Inc., 1998.

Kirby, Kimberly, Editor. "Journal of Substance Abuse Treatment." Elsevier, 2007.

Lane, Patrick. *What the stones remember: a life rediscovered*. Boston: Shambhala Publications, Inc., 2006.

Levine, Noah. *Against the stream: a buddhist manual for spiritual revolutionaries*. New York: HarperCollins Publishers, 2007.

McCloskey, Deborah and Barbara Sinor. *Addiction: what's really going on? Inside a heroin treatment program*. Ann Arbor: Loving Healing Press, 2009.

National Institute on Alcohol Abuse and Alcoholism. "Alcohol

Alert." AIAAA: Newsletter, 2009.

National Institute on Drug Abuse. *Principles of drug addiction treatment: a research based guide.* Bethesda: NIDA, 2009.

Open Society Institute. "Unforeseen Benefits: Addiction Treatment Reduces Health Care Costs" Closing the Addiction Treatment Gap, July 2009.

Orloff, Judith. *Emotional freedom.* New York: Harmony Books, 2009.

Pinsky, Drew. Interview regarding addiction in "The Oprah Magazine." New York: Heart Communications, Inc., February 2008.

Plummer, George W. *Consciously creating circumstances.* New York: Society of Rosicrucians, Inc., 1935.

Ries, Richard K., Shannon C. Miller, David A. Fielin, and Richard Saitz. *Principles of addiction medicine,* 4th Edition. Chevy Chase: American Society of Addiction Medicine, Inc., 2009.

Rodegast, Pat and Judith Stanton. *Emmanuel's book: a manual for living comfortably in the cosmos.* New York: Bantam Books, Inc., 1987.

Rogers, L. W. *Elementary theosophy.* Chicago: Theo Book Company, 1929.

Runningbear, Sage. Shaman Healer and Psychic; available for phone readings and events. Sageshamanhealer@yahoo.com.

Ruiz, Don Miguel. *The four agreements.* San Rafael: Amber-Allen Publishing, Inc., 1997.

Sams, Jamie and David Carson. *Medicine cards.* Santa Fe: Bear & Company, 1988.

Schlitz, Marilyn. "A Question of Evidence" Noetic Sciences Review, No. 34, 1995.

Schwiebert, Pat and Chuck DeKlyen. *Tear soup: a recipe for healing after loss.* Portland: Grief Watch, 1999 First Edition.

Scientific American Journal. "Reaping a Sad Harvest: A Narcotic Farm that Tried to Grow Recovery." New York: Scientific American, Inc., October 2008.

Singer, Richard A. *Eastern wisdom for your soul.* Flourtown: Dreamriver Press, 2007.

Sinor, Barbara. "Addiction: A Spiritual Journey." *Recovering The Self: A Journal of Hope and Healing.* Ann Arbor: Loving

Healing Press, Inc., Vol. 2, No. 1, January 2010.

Sinor, Barbara. "Addiction: Searching for Answers." Self-Growth.com, 2009.

Sinor, Barbara. *An inspirational guide for the recovering soul.* Upland: Astara, Inc., 2003.

Sinor, Barbara. *Gifts from the child within, 2nd Edition.* Ann Arbor: Loving Healing Press, Inc., 2008.

Slesinger, Paul A. Audio Interview by Behavioral Health Care. BHC Journal online, July 2009.

Smethers, John E. *Scumbag sewer rats: an archetypal understanding of criminalized drug addicts.* Ireland: CheckPoint Press, 2008.

Van Praagh, James. *Unfinished business: what the dead can teach us about life.* New York: HarperCollins Publishers, 2009.

Thich Nhat Hanh. *Anger: wisdom for cooling the flames.* New York: Riverhead Books, 2001.

Tolle, Eckhart. *Stillness speaks.* Novato: New World Library, 2003.

Volpicelli, Joseph and Maia Szalavitz. New York: John Wiley & Sons, Inc., 2000.

Wilber, Ken. *The integral vision.* Boston: Shambhala Publications, Inc., 2007.

Young, William P. *The shack.* Newbury Park: Windblown Media, 2007.

Zukav, Gary. *The seat of the soul.* New York: Simon & Schuster, Inc., 1999.

Recovery Resources

Addicted.org
Drug Rehab Centers in United States
www.addicted.org

Addiction Recovery Basics
www.addictionrecoverybasics.com

Addiction Resource Guide
http://www.addictionresourceguide.com/directory.html

Addiction Treatment Forum
Clinco Communications, Inc.
P.O. Box 685
Mundelein, IL 60060

Al-Anon/Alateen
www.al-anon.alateen.org

Alcoholics Anonymous®
www.alcoholics-anonymous.org
212-870-3400

**American Association for the Treatment of Opioid Dependence
(AATOD)**

225 Varick Street, 4th Floor
New York, NY 10014
212-355-4647

American Council on Alcoholism
1000 E. Indian School Road
Phoenix, AZ 85014
1-800-527-5344

American Council for Drug Education
164 West 74th Street
New York, NY 10023
1-800-488DRUG

American Society of Addiction Medicine (ASAM)
www.asam.org

Behavioral Health Care
BHC Journal
www.bhcjournal.com

The Betty Ford Center
www.bettyfordcenter.org
39000 Bob Hope Drive
Rancho Mirage, CA 92270
1-800-434-7365

Celebrate Recovery®
www.celebraterecovery.com

Centers for Disease Control & Prevention (CDC)
http://cdc.gov/
800-CDC-INFO (800-232-4636)

Center for Substance Abuse Treatment (CSAT)
Treatment Facility Locator
http://dasis3.samhsa.gov/

Center for Substance Abuse Prevention
www.samhsa.gov

Drug-Rehab-Centers
Addiction Information & Treatment
www.drug-rehab-center.org

Integral Recovery
www.integralrecovery.com
Developed by John Dupuy

Learn Genetics™
Genetic Science Learning Center
University of Utah
http://learn.genetics.utah.edu/content/addiction/drugs/mouse.html

Narcotics Anonymous
http://www.na.org

National Alliance of Medication Assisted Recovery (NAMA)
435 Second Avenue
New York, NY 10010
212-595-NAMA
nama.info@methadone.org

National Association of Alcohol, Drugs, & Disability (NAADD)
2165 Bunker Hill Drive
San Mateo, CA 94402-3801

National Association of Drug Court Professionals (NADCP)
www.nadcp.org
4900 Seminary Road
Alexandria, Virginia 22310

National Association of State Alcohol & Drug Abuse Directors (NASADAD)
1025 Connecticut Avenue NW, Suite 605
Washington, DC 20036
202-293-0090

National Center on Addiction and Substance Abuse (CASA)
www.casacolumbia.org
633 Third Avenue,
19th Floor
New York, NY 10017-6706

National Council on Alcoholism and Drug Dependence (NCADD)
244 East 58th Street, 4th Floor
New York, NY 10022
212/269-7797

National Institute on Alcohol Abuse and Alcoholism (NIAAA)
www.NIAAA.nih.gov
5635 Fishers Lane, MSC 9304
Bethesda, MD 20892-9304
301-443-3860

National Institute on Drug Abuse (NIDA)
6001 Executive Boulevard, Room 5213
Bethesda, MD 20892-9561

Not Alone
Codependent's Guide to the 12-Steps
www.enotaline.com/article/5578.html

Open Society Institute
400 West 59th Street
New York, NY 10019
www.treatmentgap.org

Opioid Treatment Program Directory
1 Choke Cherry Road, Room 2-1075
Rockville, MD 20857
240-276-2700
otp@samhsa.hhs.gov

Sacred Space Healing and Retreat Center
Anderson Springs, CA
1-800-914-6360
www.sacredspaceretreats.com

SMART Recovery®
http://www.smartrecovery.org/

Sober Recovery
Recovery Resources Online
www.soberresources.com

Substance Abuse & Mental Health Services Administration (SAMHSA)
Health Information Network
P.O. Box 2345
Rockville, MD 20847-2345
http://www.samhsa.gov/shin

About the Author

Barbara Sinor, Ph.D. is a Psychospiritual Therapist dealing with childhood abuse/incest, PTSD, addiction recovery, and adult children of alcoholics. Dr. Sinor uses integral holistic methods encompassing forms of hypnotherapy, regression therapy, Jungian dreamwork, and other transpersonal techniques. Dr. Sinor holds a Doctorate in Psychology, a Master of Arts from John F. Kennedy University, and her Bachelor of Arts degree is from Pitzer College of the Claremont Colleges.

Dr. Sinor encourages your comments and can be contacted through her web site at www.DrSinor.com. Her work also appears in the quarterly *Recovering The Self: A Journal of Hope and Healing*.

Others books by Dr. Sinor:

Beyond Words: A Lexicon of Metaphysical Thought
Gifts from the Child Within
An Inspirational Guide for the Recovering Soul
Addiction—What's Really Going On? Inside a Heroin Treatment Program (co-author Deborah McCloskey)

About the Cover

In the spring of 2008, Barbara's afternoon walk led her to a shallow area of the private lake within her Northern California community. Not believing a usable picture would come from positioning the little digital camera just inches from the water, she captured an image which was later to be the cover of this book. Barbara's interpretation of her photograph is that it covertly represents the many levels of emotional sinking, floating, and rising above the challenges those with an addiction face on their recovery journey.

Index